PICTORIAL HISTORY
OF THE R.A.F.

PICTORIAL HISTORY OF
THE R.A.F.

Volume 3 . 1945-1969

J. W. R. TAYLOR
AND
P. J. R. MOYES

LONDON

IAN ALLAN

First published 1970

SBN 7110 0132 4

© Ian Allan 1970

Published by Ian Allan Ltd., Shepperton, Surrey, and printed in the United Kingdom
by The Press at Coombelands Ltd., Addlestone, Surrey.

Contents

Introduction

In this volume, our brief history of the first half-century of the Royal Air Force is completed. We see the service reaching a peak of strength that even its creator, Lord Trenchard, would never have believed possible. To the immense power of the H-bomb is added the unrivalled capability of the V-bombers, producing an offensive force that could, by itself, have eliminated 80 per cent of all worthwhile targets in the Soviet Union.

This was a force so mighty that it never had to be used, and the world was able to enjoy a quarter-century of comparative peace in a period when World War III often seemed a daily possibility. Yet, because there was no need to send the V-bombers into action, politicians were unable to appreciate their value and for thirteen disastrous years the potential of the Royal Air Force was degraded by repeated wrong decisions and indecision until even its friends began to see it as a service without any obvious purpose, direction or firm plans for the future.

Year after year, the aircraft that the R.A.F. wanted were denied it; the aircraft it was allowed to order were, in many cases, products of political expediency rather than sound military planning. Fortunately, the very emptiness of such a policy has given an opportunity for redress. A new government, with a mandate to give the people value for money or to get out, never to return, must determine precisely what is required to give the R.A.F. the world-wide prestige it enjoyed in 1945 and the power it possessed in 1965. Having decided what is needed, it must ensure that the R.A.F. gets it. The ultimate cost will not prove excessive. Economically, only good will come from encouraging our aircraft industry to utilise its know-how to probe the limits of technological possibility. Politically, strength is still respected and World War III will continue to be averted only so long as both East and West maintain the clear capability of annihilating each other.

One day, perhaps, men from the little-minded, nothing-much-to-lose nations, who create so much of the present world tension and unhappiness, may share with Americans and Russians the ability to look across the wilderness of space at the green and lovely oasis of Earth. They will then see all men as one, on a planet that could offer plenty for all and should offer peace to all. At the dawn of the 'seventies this seems like a dream incapable of fulfilment; yet the choice that lies before us has never been so clear-cut—we can continue striving for ultimate peace or ultimate destruction.

Even the choice may remain valid only if Britain remains strong while so much of the world is weak. That, above all, is the lesson that emerges from a study of what the Royal Air Force has achieved in fifty years.

August, 1970   J.W.R.T. and P.J.R.M.

Chapter One

From Hot War to Cold

Once I said to Field-Marshal Konev (Soviet High Commissioner for Austria), "You've made ten demands at this Council meeting that we can't meet. But suppose I should say, 'All right. We agree to all ten demands.' Then what would you do?"
"Tomorrow," he said, "I'd have ten new ones."

General Mark Clark. Calculated Risk.

WORLD WAR II had ended. After six seemingly-endless, wearisome years it was almost impossible to believe, except by those able to welcome home husbands and sons from enemy prisoner-of-war camps.

The return from captivity had begun in April 1945, when R.A.F. Dakotas, Stirlings and Halifaxes of Nos. 38 and 46 Groups had brought back to England 27,277 newly-released British and American prisoners, after ferrying 7,500 tons of fuel, oil and ammunition to the Second Tactical Air Force on the outward flights. By June, when the German camps were empty, Bomber Command alone had carried home 75,000 men. In addition, between April 29th and May 8th, some 250 of the aircraft that had devastated Germany with bombs showered food on the starving people of Holland.

A few months later, when Japan too had surrendered unconditionally, the errands of mercy were repeated. This time the needs were even more desperate, and the scenes at prisoner-of-war camps even more heartbreaking, for the Japanese had treated their hundred thousand military and civilian captives with a callousness that westerners found difficult to comprehend.

Before repatriation could begin, 33 million leaflets had to be dropped over 90 prison camps and 150 other areas of Malaya, Thailand, Indo-China, Java and Sumatra, informing friend and foe alike that the war was over and telling the captives that they would soon be freed. Under Operations Birdcage and Mastiff, airborne medical teams were dropped into the camps, together with

9

radio operators who could advise immediately of the most urgent requirements.

Food and clothing were parachuted to the former prisoners, mostly by aircraft from the Cocos Islands where depots were kept stocked by pressing into service every available Liberator bomber and Sunderland flying-boat. Every week a million tablets of Atabrine were dropped from one Dakota and nine Liberator squadrons, as protection against malaria. And all the time prisoners were flown to freedom, including 9,000 survivors of the men who had suffered the ordeal of working on the Siam-Burma railway.

Perhaps, even at this moment of supreme relief and thankfulness, it would have been better for the whole world had it listened more attentively to the fears expressed by Winston Churchill. Four days after the German surrender, he had sent a telegram to President Truman of America recording his profound concern over the situation developing in Europe. After noting the rapidly-vanishing Allied forces on the continent, he wrote:

"Meanwhile, what is to happen about Russia? I have always worked for friendship with Russia, but, like you, I feel deep anxiety because of their misinterpretation of the Yalta decisions, their attitude towards Poland, their overwhelming influence in the Balkans, excepting Greece, the difficulties they make about Vienna, the combination of Russian power and the territories under their control or occupied, coupled with the Communist technique in so many other countries, and above all their power to maintain very large armies in the field for a long time. . . .

"An iron curtain is drawn down upon their front. We do not know what is going on behind . . . and it would be open to the Russians in a very short time to advance if they chose to the waters of the North Sea and the Atlantic. Surely it is vital now to come to an understanding with Russia, or see where we are with her, before we weaken our armies mortally or retire to the zones of occupation . . ."

Such warnings were not welcome to the British people of the time. Weary of war, primed with propaganda about the achievements of their Soviet allies who had swept through Eastern Europe to Berlin, eager to taste the sweet fruits of victory rather than any more of Winston's standard offering of "blood, toil, sweat and tears" on which they had persisted for so long, they swept him from power in a general election on July 25th, even before Japan had been defeated, and replaced him with his wartime deputy, Clement Attlee.

At the time they did so, British prestige and foreign respect for this nation had never stood higher. The Royal Air Force, with which we are concerned here, had ended the last month of the war in Europe with no fewer than 55,469 aircraft, of which the 9,200 in front-line service had played a major, easily-recognised role in the achievement of a great victory. How fleeting are fame and fortune – especially when nobody seems to care as they melt away.

As the strength of the British armed forces was eroded by demobilisation, and the "Empire on which the sun never sets" disintegrated under the influence of Socialism in London and nationalism overseas, it gradually became clear that the lessons of the 'twenties had been forgotten. Intent on developing an idealistic welfare state, the Labour Government in London concentrated its efforts on the social services and sought every possible economy in other directions.

The pattern for the post-war R.A.F. was set in March 1946, when John Strachey, Under-Secretary of State for Air, presented to Parliament the Air Estimates. He said, among other things, that 742,000 persons, out of the R.A.F.'s strength of 1,100,000 at the end of the war with Germany, would have been released by June 30th, 1946, and that six months later the Service would be down to about 305,000 total strength.

America had the atomic bomb and a huge bomber force with which to deliver it. Why then, should Britain go to the expense of developing anything better than the piston-engined Lincoln, an evolution of the wartime Lancaster which it was replacing in Bomber Command?

In vain was it emphasised by those with less-rose-tinted spectacles that the actions of America in the political field were, to say the very least, unpredictable and that it was essential to maintain a balanced defensive/offensive air force. Even Fighter Command was left in no doubt that it would have to make do with improved versions of wartime fighters for many years to come.

In view of the lead in jet propulsion which Britain's aircraft industry had among allied nations at the end of the war, this might have seemed a safe course. Only the R.A.F. Meteor had been operated in squadron service, and the American aero-engine and airframe industries were gaining their early jet experience by utilising turbojets of basic British design. Unfortunately, Mr. Attlee's men made two major mistakes at this moment, one of which by good fortune did not have serious consequences. The other did.

After the German collapse, teams of highly-qualified Service and civilian personnel had visited captured airfields and factories to study and report on enemy progress in aircraft and missile development. Some of the projects they uncovered were almost unbelievably advanced and bizarre—like the Bachem Natter piloted rocket-powered interceptor, designed to be launched vertically from a ramp; a Messerschmitt fighter with a "swing-wing"; a Focke-Wulf fighter with a three-blade rotor that turned axially around the aircraft's fuselage to combine vertical take-off with high cruising speed; and another project which utilised a pre-heated block of carbon inserted into a duct in the fuselage as an utterly simple jet-type power plant.

Such seeming flights of fancy could be disregarded safely in terms of immediate applications; but it was stupid to ignore the results of German research which showed unmistakably the advantages of using sweptback wings. Years earlier, the first encounters with compressibility effects—shock-waves created by airflow over an aircraft approaching the speed of sound—had led to immense problems with the Typhoon fighter and had initiated development of the Tempest with "thin" wings to slow the airflow and so delay the onset of compressibility. The Germans had discovered that by sweeping back the wings of their aircraft this problem could be further offset, permitting still higher speeds.

Not only did the British government decide that it was unnecessary to take advantage of this research for the jet aircraft that would be flown by the post-war R.A.F.; they also decided that it was too dangerous to continue the programme under which the Miles M.52 research aircraft was to attempt to break through the "sound barrier" to a speed of 1,000 m.p.h.

On July 18th, 1946, Sir Ben Lockspeiser, Director General of Scientific Research (Air), told the press: "Flying at speeds greater than that of sound* introduces new problems. We do not yet know how serious they are. The impression that supersonic aircraft are just round the corner is quite erroneous. But the difficulties will be tackled by the use of rocket-driven models. We have not the heart to ask pilots to fly the high-speed models, so we shall make them radio-controlled."

Just over a year later, on October 14th, 1947, the futility of playing with rocket models was underlined when Major Charles E. Yeager of the U.S.A.F. become the first pilot to exceed the speed of sound, in the rocket-powered Bell X-1 research aircraft. Britain's Service and test pilots, while congratulating the Americans on a great achievement, felt bitter that a stupid government decision should have robbed this country of so important a "first".

---

* 760 m.p.h. at sea level, falling to 660 m.p.h. above 36,000 ft.

By that time, both the United States and Russia had built prototype fighters embodying German ideas on sweptwing design. The North American XP-86 Sabre flew on October 1st, 1947, and exceeded Mach 1 (the speed of sound) for the first time in a shallow dive a few months later, on April 26th.

The Soviet MiG-15 was in a less happy position at first, as its engine-makers had not been able to benefit from British "know-how" and it was designed around a rather inadequate German wartime engine. Then in 1946, to its eternal shame, the Labour government agreed to sell to Russia 25 Rolls-Royce Nene and 30 Rolls-Royce Derwent engines. Suffice it to say that when the MiG-15 prototype flew for the first time on December 30th, 1947, it did so on the unrivalled power of a Nene. Subsequently, V. Y. Klimov evolved improved versions of this engine for the production MiG-15, MiG-17 and Il-28 bomber, the aircraft on which the whole concept of modern Soviet tactical air power was founded.

Back in the early post-war period, the leaders of the R.A.F. could only anticipate gloomily the possible future fruits of official policy and put on a brave face by demonstrating the quality of their current personnel, equipment and training.

On May 16th, 1945, little more than a week after the end of the war in Europe, the Lancaster *Aries* of the Empire Air Navigation School, Shawbury, set out for training flights over the true North and Magnetic North Poles. It returned from White Horse, Yukon, on May 26th, in 18 hours, 26 minutes, completing a total of 17,720 miles.

This was but the first of many fine navigation exercises by *Aries* and its successors, pointing the way to commercial air routes fo the future, over the polar regions. More exciting for the popular press were attempts on the world's absolute speed record by Meteor fighters which demonstrated clearly the great increase in performance brought by the transition from piston-engines to jets.

Throughout the war years, the record had remained officially at the figure of 469.22 m.p.h. set up by Fritz Wendel in a Messerschmitt Me 209 on April 26th, 1939. It was easy to exceed this in a Meteor; so two standard production F.Mk.3's were prepared for the task. Radio, aerials and guns were removed, and the gun blast-tubes faired over. Fuel capacity was brought up to 375 gallons by installing an extra tank in the empty ammunition bay, and the aircraft were made deliberately tail heavy to prevent any possibility of a sudden dive into the sea during speed runs over a course at Herne Bay, Kent.

On November 7th, 1945, Group Captain H. J. Wilson, one of the

R.A.F.'s most experienced jet pilots, raised the record to a dazzling 606.38 m.p.h. in one of these Meteors (EE454 *Britannia*). It seemed just possible that America might beat this with a hotted-up P-80 Shooting Star fighter; so an R.A.F. High Speed Flight was formed on June 14th, 1946, to push the record higher.

Two cleaned-up Meteor F.Mk.4's, with specially-boosted 4,200 lb. thrust Derwent engines, were allocated to the Flight, and on September 7th Group Captain E. M. Donaldson averaged 615.778 m.p.h. in one of them (EE549) over a course between Rustington and Angmering on the South Coast. It was a fine achievement, but remained unbeaten for only nine months, and Britain has since held this supreme record for only two comparatively brief periods in nearly a quarter of a century. During this period, the country's airframe industry has lost none of its world-leading ability, while its engine manufacturers have continued to set the pace for others to follow. Disappointments and frustrations have resulted largely from lack of vision by successive governments.

Twenty-five years is a long period—half of the lifetime of the Royal Air Force as this is being written. It has been free of major war only because the terrifying power of the atomic bomb was demonstrated by the *actual use* of two of these weapons against Japan in August 1945. Unfortunately, this has been a case of "peace through fear"—the fear of nuclear annihilation—with little evidence of any universal desire for co-existence between nations, and there has hardly been a moment when the R.A.F. was not fighting a "minor" war somewhere or other.

World War II had left Britain with commitments all over the world; and it was soon clear that peace and stability would be but dreams in the face of seething nationalism, often encouraged by our former Communist allies, who also had designs on territorial expansion.

In addition to the four operational commands (Bomber, Fighter, Coastal, Transport) and four non-operational Commands (Flying Training, Technical Training, Maintenance and Reserve) at home, the R.A.F. had more than a dozen overseas Commands immediately after the war. There were the British Air Forces of Occupation in Germany; the R.A.F. in Northern Ireland and Gibraltar; Headquarters Austria, Greece, Italy, Malta, Aden, East Africa, Iraq and Levant under the R.A.F. Mediterranean and Middle East Command; Headquarters Burma, Ceylon, Hong Kong, Malaya and Singapore under Air Command South-East Asia; Air Headquarters West Africa; and R.A.F. India.

To maintain its peace-keeping roles, the Royal Air Force was allocated £255½ million under the 1946 Defence Estimates, £214 million in 1947 and £173 million in 1948. Under the burden of such dwindling resources, its power shrunk gradually to a little more than 1,000 first-line aircraft in 100 under-strength squadrons, manned by 38,000 regular personnel and a mass of short-term conscripts. Lack of funds was to delay the total re-equipment with jets of day fighter squadrons until 1950; the last of the night fighter squadrons had to be patient until 1952. All bomber squadrons continued to fly on piston-engines until mid-1951.

Almost the only bright spots were an announcement on June 2nd, 1946, that the Auxiliary Air Force was to be re-formed with 13 day fighter (Spitfire), three night fighter (Mosquito) and four light bomber (Mosquito) squadrons, followed by confirmation of the R.A.F. Regiment as an integral part of the peacetime Service on July 10th, and reintroduction of R.A.F. Volunteer Reserve air centres and the University Air Squadrons.

The men who controlled these forces brought immense experience to the task. Chief of the Air Staff from January 1st, 1946, was Marshal of the Royal Air Force Sir Arthur Tedder, who had been General Eisenhower's Deputy Supreme Commander for the invasion of Europe in 1944, after commanding the Middle East and Mediterranean Air Forces. Bomber Command was headed by Air Marshal Sir Hugh Saunders, a wartime fighter leader who had later commanded the R.A.F. in Burma. Fighter Command came under Air Marshal Sir James Robb, another great "fighter boy" who had been Eisenhower's Chief of Staff (Air) in 1944–45. Such was the calibre of the men who, to paraphrase Winston Churchill, had to achieve so much with so little and so few.

The troubles started even before Tedder took over from Marshal of the R.A.F. Lord Portal. Freed of the Japanese invaders, the people of the Netherlands East Indies decided that the time had come to get rid also of Dutch control. Proclaiming the existence of the state of Indonesia, they clashed with troops of the British South East Asia Command who were rounding up the Japanese. When they murdered the commanding officer of the 49th Indian Infantry Brigade, Brigadier S. W. S. Mallaby, it was clearly time for the R.A.F. to go back into action.

On November 9th, 1945, Mosquitos of Nos. 84 and 110 Squadrons began armed reconnaissance sorties, ready to use their guns and bombs if required. On the 15th they were joined by five aircraft of No. 82 Squadron—the first "Mossies" deployed in the Far East with rocket armament, which had been seen previously only on Beau-fighters—and then by more rocket-firing Mosquitos of No. 47 Squadron.

First to see combat in the new trouble spot, on November 17th, was No. 47. It despatched four aircraft against a radio station near Kemajoran which was playing a major part in inciting the rebels, and followed it with a similar attack on Soeramarta radio station eight days later. On the 26th, three aircraft of No. 84 Squadron struck at rebel units in the Ambarawa region. Simultaneously, four Mosquitos from Nos. 47 and 84 Squadrons attacked the radio station at Tagjakarta, after the occupants had been forewarned by leaflets showered from a Beaufighter.

Other R.A.F. Squadrons which took part in these operations were No. 60, with Thunderbolts, and No. 155, with Spitfires, which attacked Surabaya radio station under the guidance of Austers of No. 656 (Air Observation Post) Squadron. This particular station was the home of "Surabaya Sue", who poured out a stream of anti-British propaganda. Its silencing was achieved at the cost of damage to some of the Austers caused by rifle fire from the ground.

Patrols to cover British troop movements continued through December, mainly by 47 Squadron, which fired 24 rockets into a troublesome road block near Kampong on the 21st. Escort and reconnaissance duties were maintained until January 20th, but no further offensive action was required and the operation was regarded as completed on March 12th.

It was not the end of the troubles in the islands. The rebels had siezed Japanese weapons and even a few ex-enemy aircraft which they used against the Dutch. These were soon shot down, or destroyed on the ground, but the anti-colonialist movement was well under way by now.

On July 18th, 1947, the imminent break-up of the British Empire was signalled when the Indian independence bill became law. It was followed on August 15th by establishment of the two separate, completely independent Dominions of Pakistan and India, with attendant migrations, and massacres. Two years later, on December 27th, 1949, sovereignty over the former Dutch East Indies passed to the new Republic of the United States of Indonesia, except for the western part of New Guinea (West Irian).

If anyone expected peace and contentment to follow such fulfil-ment of national aspirations, they were to be sadly disillusioned. Nor was the United Nations Organisation, set up so hopefully by the victors after World War II, to prove effective, because there never was any unity of thoughts, hopes or moral standards among the steadily-growing number of signatories.

Everywhere, Communism clashed with the western concepts of democracy, with an uncompromising coldness and deliberateness that is typified by the quotation on page 9 from the memoirs of General Mark Clark, U.S. High Commissioner in Austria. What little remained of wartime camaraderie melted away. Winston Churchill's "Iron Curtain" across Europe became increasingly impenetrable, and it began to seem as if World War III was being averted only by America's exclusive possession of nuclear weapons.

Were even these sufficient to avoid a final suicidal clash between the two great power groups of East and West? The world breathed a little easier as the Greek government stamped out Communist attempts to take over their country by force; but it was at the western approaches to Berlin, an isolated city under four-power control, completely surrounded by Communist East Germany, that the real danger to the future of humanity soon became terribly apparent.

B

Chapter Two

Vittles and Plainfare

The Russians were underestimating the resource and resolution of the Western Allies and the Western Sector Germans. Hugh McManus, the little Scottish platoon sergeant, had told his German wife, Irmgard, that whatever the Russians did the British would do something better, and he was right.

Robert Rodrigo. *Berlin Airlift.*

BERLIN COULD HARDLY have avoided being a trouble-spot. Agreements between the victorious allied nations had left it under four-power military government, with the eastern half of the city under Russian control and with America, Britain and France responsible for the western half.

There were 2,100,000 Germans in western Berlin, plus a few thousand allied troops and civil servants, and a handful of welfare workers and journalists. Even if life had been allowed to go on as smoothly as possible, their situation was unenviable. The former German capital had been devastated by bombing; its public services were largely wrecked and its industry virtually at a standstill in 1945. Even worse, it was an "island", about 100 miles inside the Russian zone of a divided Germany.

Three post-war years had brought only slow improvement by 1948. The Russian "iron curtain" foreseen by Winston Churchill had fallen between the whole of eastern and western Europe. Expedient wartime cooperation had given way to suspicion, frustration and deliberate provocation, in a non-shooting "cold war". Both halves of Berlin remained drab and depressing. If the western sector progressed more rapidly than its Russian-controlled neighbour, it was only a relative improvement. Unemployed men and black marketeers were everywhere, while women did much of the hard work like pushing rail-trolleys filled with rubble from the streets and shattered buildings. The city was kept alive and barely at work at the cost of 13,500 tons

18

of food, coal, raw materials and other goods that flowed in daily by rail, road and water.

It seemed to the Russians that they could remove the unwanted presence of their late allies from west Berlin simply by cutting these transport arteries and refusing to restore them until the whole of the city had been put under their control. It was the sort of blackmail that usually worked. They were confident that the U.S.A., then sole deployer of nuclear weapons, would never resort to the use of such means of total war just to retain part of a wrecked ex-enemy city; and they could think of no other practicable way of forcing them to lift their projected blockade. It was all rather simple . . .

So, early in 1948, the squeeze started. Petty restrictions were imposed which made it difficult for people from the western sectors to enter their zone to barter for food. By the spring, it was ruled that no freight would be allowed to pass from the city to the western zones of Germany without Soviet permission. When subsequent searches of westbound passenger trains met with resistance from Britain and America, the trains were delayed endlessly at the frontier.

On June 18th, Marshal Sokolovsky, Soviet Military Governor in Berlin, issued a statement decrying allied plans for currency reforms in western Germany and forbidding circulation of the new money in Berlin or the Russian zone. On the same day, the Russians ordered that all passenger train movements between the western and Soviet zones, and all motor traffic on the road linking Berlin with the west, should cease at midnight.

Rail traffic on the Berlin-Helmstedt line, the city's only remaining rail link with the west, was suspended on the pretext of "technical troubles" on the 24th. Barge traffic had been stopped three days earlier, on the day that Russia had announced its own plan for currency reform in east Germany and the whole of Berlin. In one last attempt at compromise, the western allies agreed to recognise the eastern currency, even if their own "new marks" were rejected. At that moment, electricity supplies to their zone, from power stations in the east, were cut drastically. It seemed symbolic of the growing gloom, as Russia sat back to await the handing over to it of responsibility for the entire city—now cut off completely except for some rather pathetic air corridors.

Establishment of the air corridors had been one of the few significant points of agreement reached in all the four-power meetings. It provided for three air routes into Berlin from the western zones, each 20 miles wide, converging like an arrow-head into an air traffic control zone extending out 20 miles from the Allied Control Council building in the city. Aircraft had to fly no higher than 10,000 feet, and the insecurity of the whole arrangement had been emphasised on April 5th, 1948 by a collision between a passenger-carrying Viking airliner of British European Airways and a Soviet Yakovlev fighter inside the control zone, in which all the occupants of both aircraft were killed.

The northern corridor led in a south-easterly direction from Hamburg and the central corridor due east from Hanover, both in the British zone. The longer southern corridor extended in a north-easterly direction from near Frankfurt, in the American zone. All three funnelled their traffic into Berlin's main Tempelhof Airport, in the U.S. sector of the city, and the former *Luftwaffe* training centre of Gatow, in the British sector near the Havel lake.

Only a few passenger aircraft normally plodded daily down these routes, carrying tiny quantities of freight and mail. However, both America and Britain had worked out plans to ferry essential supplies by air along the corridors, to meet the requirements of their own nationals in Berlin on a short-term basis, if Soviet intransigence should ever make such a move necessary. America had put this scheme into effect from April 1st, 1948. The R.A.F. eventually followed suit, by sending 16 Dakotas to the airfield of Wunstorf, at the western end of the centre corridor, with the aim of flying 65 tons of freight into Berlin each day, under Operation Knicker. The origin of the code-name is not recorded, but soldiers of the Royal Army Service Corps who were flown into the city to handle unloading of the aircraft were told that the job was so urgent that, if they were stopped by Military Police, all they had to do was pronounce the word "Knicker" and they would pass unchallenged. One of them immediately obtained from an undisclosed source a garment corresponding to the pass-word and displayed it on his car as a banner to ensure the quickest possible service.

When the Soviet blockade became complete, the U.S.A.F. conceived the far more ambitious idea of trying to feed the entire population of the western half of the city. Under the operational code-name "Vittles", it assembled a fleet of twin-engined C-47 (Dakota) transports at Wiesbaden Air Force Base and began despatching them in a continuous stream up the southern corridor to Tempelhof, each laden with three short tons of supplies.

This was the sort of challenge the R.A.F. could accept with relish, even in its depleted state. From Headquarters No. 46 Group of R.A.F. Transport Command, at Watford in Hertfordshire,

Operation Order No. 9 was issued on June 30th, 1948, to reflect a Cabinet decision. It stated, uncompromisingly:

"1. Following the breakdown of the surface communications between the British Zone of GERMANY and the British Sector in BERLIN, the latter will be supplied completely by air.

2. The airlift into BERLIN is to be built up as rapidly as possible to 400 tons per day and maintained at that level until 3rd July, 1948. Therefrom it is to be increased to 750 tons per day by 7th July, 1948.

3. In Phase I up to 3rd July inclusive, Dakotas of 46 and 38 Groups operating under the control and direction of Air Headquarters, British Air Forces of Occupation (Germany) will provide the 400 tons per day lift."

They were intended to be supplemented by the four-engined Yorks of 47 Group for Phase II.

Meanwhile, events had been moving fast at Wunstorf. At a staff conference on June 24th, the station commander had revealed that the place was about to be invaded by transport squadrons, so his three fighter squadrons would have to disappear elsewhere—quickly! Eight Dakotas arrived from England next day and began flying down the corridor to Gatow, without payloads, to study the route. Every available space in the station buildings was filled with beds and bunks. Lashed by rain and high winds, the R.A.S.C. put up a village of tents at the edge of the airfield. Then, within 24 hours some 200 tons of flour and meat were poured into Wunstorf, together with German civilian labour to help the troops.

Between June 28th and 30th, about 75 tons of food were carried to Gatow in 20 flights, mostly for the British garrison. Then the build-up began in earnest. When five Dakotas of No. 30 Squadron flew into Wunstorf from Oakington, in Cambridgeshire, it took their crews an hour to find somewhere to park. On July 1st, the tonnage of freight flown into Berlin totalled 405, more than three-quarters of it for German civilians. Operation Carter Paterson had taken over from, and absorbed, Knicker.

The change of code-name was not a happy one. The Russians, with rare humour, lost no time in explaining through press and radio that, as Carter Paterson was the name of a well-known British removals firm, this implied that the R.A.F. had been given the task of removing as much as possible from Berlin before the inevitable allied departure from the city. To prevent any misunderstanding among the folk they were trying to help, the R.A.F. promptly switched to a more appropriate Operation Plainfare.

By this time, there were 48 Dakotas at Wunstorf, belonging to Nos. 30, 46, 53, 77 and 238 Squadrons and No. 240 O.C.U. The first Yorks arrived on July 2nd and by the middle of the month there were so many of them that it was decided to transfer all the Dakotas to Fassberg, a few miles to the north-east. From there they began carrying sacks of coal into Berlin on July 19th—probably the first and perhaps the only time in history that such a bulky, low-value cargo has been air-freighted continuously over a lengthy period. Economics were of far less importance than the survival of those to whom it was flown.

The Yorks came into their own from July 16th, when completion of a new concrete runway at Gatow enabled them to be used to full capacity. There were eventually seven squadrons of them on the airlift, and they carried nearly half of all the cargoes flown in R.A.F. aircraft; but they were by no means the only British "heavies" used in Plainfare.

Within 24 hours of somebody suggesting that the flying-boats of Coastal Command might operate a valuable supply operation between a base on the river Elbe, near Hamburg, and Havel Lake, the first Sunderlands arrived in Germany on July 4th. Theirs was to be no easy task. The Elbe was still littered with the wreckage of ships that had been sunk during the war; and they had to moor in an exposed stretch of water, with their "operations room" housed in riverside marquees.

Despite all the difficulties, the Sunderlands of Nos. 201 and 230 squadrons made more than 1,000 flights into Berlin between July 5th and December 15th, when ice at Havel brought this phase of Plainfare to a halt. The sight of these huge, graceful machines banking over their city and landing on their beloved lake gave the Berliners a special thrill. Because of the Sunderlands' anti-corrosion protection against sea water, they were for a time the only aircraft able to carry urgently-needed salt. Their operation was made particularly slick by the use of DUKW amphibious vehicles for loading and unloading, and turn-round times were reduced to 20 minutes at Hamburg and only 12 minutes in Berlin. Altogether, they carried 4,500 tons of food into the city and brought out 1,113 undernourished children for treatment in the west.

By the end of July, the first full month of the airlift, civilian charter aircraft began arriving to supplement the weight of cargoes that could be carried daily, under R.A.F. control. First on the scene were two ex-T.C.A. Lancastrians, veterans of scores of transatlantic flights but now operating as fuel tankers in the service of Flight Refuelling Ltd. They began flying into Gatow on July 27th, ten days ahead of the date set for the official opening of the Civil Air Lift organised by B.E.A. Before long they were joined by two Avro Tudor 25 tankers belonging to Air Vice Marshal D. C. T. Bennett's Airflight Ltd., each fitted out to carry ten short tons of fuel oil in five 500-gallon tanks. Their owner, best remembered as the leader of the R.A.F.'s wartime Pathfinder Force, showed he had lost none of his old skill when he took off from Gatow one day in G-AKBY with the elevator control locks in place. With only the trim-tabs available for pitch control, he made a steady circuit and landed safely.

Other civil types which flew side-by-side with the R.A.F. included Tudors of British South American Airways, Dakotas, Liberators, Vikings, Haltons, Halifaxes, Bristol Freighters and three ex-B.O.A.C. Hythe flying-boats which Wing Commander Barry Aikman operated into Havel lake alongside the R.A.F. Sunderlands. Owned by 25 different companies, this assortment of types contributed an invaluable 59,796 flying hours to the operation and did several highly-specialised jobs that would have been difficult for the Service aircraft. The Haltons (evolved from Halifax bombers) for example, could take over the carriage of salt, as their freight panniers were built into the former bomb-bay, well away from where the salt could do much damage. But the civil aircraft are really outside the scope of this book.

Meanwhile, the Americans had called in four-engined C-54 Skymaster squadrons from every part of the world, to take over from the C-47's and increase greatly the weight and volume of freight carried on each flight. Soon they had so many Skymasters that their two airfields at Wiesbaden and Rhein/Main (Frankfurt) were saturated. Many of them were, therefore, put on the coal lift from Fassberg in the British zone. Soon, this airfield became so crowded that it was handed over completely to the U.S.A.F., its R.A.F. and civilian Dakotas being moved north to an aerodrome near Lübeck.

To accommodate the larger American aircraft, the R.A.F. performed outstanding feats of airfield construction at Fassberg, repeating the job soon afterwards at nearby Celle, which was used only by U.S.A.F. Skymasters, though always administered and commanded by the R.A.F. At the receiving end of the supplies, the Americans and French built a completely new terminal at Tegel, in the French sector of Berlin, which came into use as the city's third airlift airfield in the autumn of 1948.

A further move, in October, saw all the civilian aircraft transferred to Fuhlsbuttel, the former airport of Hamburg; and one more northern-corridor base came into the picture in the following month, when No. 47 Squadron began operating Handley Page Hastings C.1.'s, the R.A.F.'s first transports of post-war design, from Schleswigland. It was joined later by a second Hastings squadron, No. 297, and these units left little doubt of the potential of Transport Command's York replacement, even if their first major assignment was merely as coal trucks.

As the long days of summer gave way to autumn and winter, and the number of aircraft engaged continued to grow, the airlift changed from daylight-only to a 24-hour operation. It had started almost lightheartedly, by crews who believed they were going on a short detachment that would provide good training for future sustained combat supply operations. Now, Plainfare and Vittles had settled into a businesslike, relentless routine that seemed as if it could, and might, go on for ever.

Aircraft from Wiesbaden and Rhein/Main continued to fly up the southern corridor, but returned down the centre one. All other aircraft entered Berlin via the northern corridor and also returned by the centre one, except for the Fuhlsbuttel and Schleswigland machines which were routed back along the northerly edge of the northern route. The careful navigation so essential to stay within the corridors was aided by medium-frequency radio beacons and Eureka radar beacons on the northern and central routes, with GCA (ground controlled approach) talk-down installations for blind landings in bad weather at most of the airfields. All the R.A.F. transports were also equipped to utilise the Gee radar chain set up during the World War II advance across Germany.

Control was difficult, as the efficiency of the whole operation depended on having the aircraft arriving in a steady stream over Berlin, to land at intervals of three to five minutes; yet the various types flew at different speeds and were fed into the northern corridor from six airfields. Safety was ensured by despatching the transports in groups of twelve to twenty machines of similar speed at fixed heights, with a horizontal separation of $7\frac{1}{2}$ miles between slower aircraft and 9 miles between faster types. At any one period, therefore, the northern corridor might have contained five streams of Hastings, Skymasters, Yorks, Lancastrians, Tudors and Dakotas, at different levels between 1,500 and 5,500 ft., heading from Schleswigland and Fassberg to Tegel, and from Wunstorf, Celle and Lübeck to Gatow, with Haltons returning from Tegel to Schleswigland at 1,000 ft. The faster machines could overtake the slower ones en route, which again complicated matters in the Berlin control zone. It would have been a test of calm efficiency under ideal conditions. In the rain, mud and autumn fogs of 1948 it was miraculous.

Inevitably, there were accidents, but most were trivial. Army and civilian drivers, unused to working near anything that could be so easily damaged as an aeroplane, drove petrol bowsers or lorries too near to wingtips, ailerons or pitot heads. An instrument repairer stood on a signal pistol, which fired and set light to a York. Such incidents, and engine failure in flight, accounted for most of the 27 mishaps to R.A.F. aircraft in the first month of the airlift. Then and later, there were many near accidents, avoided by good aircraft and fine flying, as when Flying Officer Cooke took off in a Dakota from Wunstorf carrying a five-ton load intended for a York.

When the end of the story was more tragic, the Soviet authorities sometimes proved strangely sympathetic. In the case of two R.A.F. machines and one civil transport which crashed in their zone, they waived all formalities and let through Service medical teams, and even the wife of one dying officer, to visit the scene of the accidents. But it was difficult to forget that the airlift that had become so essential would have been unnecessary from the start had those apparently humane people been willing to live in friendship with former allies.

Month by month the tonnage of food and equipment flown into the beleaguered city increased in quantity and variety. Food, fuel and medical supplies always had top priority, but other cargoes ranged from a steam roller, carried in pieces, to clothes, cutlery, cigarettes and calculating machines. Between June 26th and the end of July 1948, the combined U.S./British total had been 70,241 tons in 14,036 flights. By the month of December this weight doubled in only 2,450 more sorties, because of the switch to larger aircraft. By May 1949, it was possible to fly in a record 250,794 tons in 27,717 flights in a month. The British contribution was 58,547 tons in 8,352 flights.

West Berlin, incredibly, was still alive and at work. Some homes were lit by candles. Housewives had learned new tricks of cooking with easy-to-fly foods like powdered potato and dried eggs. A German cartoonist drew the best joke of the airlift, depicting the arrival of a stork in the home of a young Berlin couple, bearing a package labelled "Dehydrated baby; soak for 20 minutes in warm water."

The Russians were defeated and they knew it. Instead of bombs, the R.A.F. and U.S.A.F. had won a great victory with unarmed transport aircraft. At one minute past midnight on May 11-12th, the blockade was lifted. The airlift was to be maintained until October, to build up stocks in the western sectors of Berlin; but the Russians were to retreat behind a wall built as a physical barrier to keep out people and ideas.

By the end, the R.A.F. had flown in a total of 394,509 short tons of cargo in 65,857 sorties. At the peak of the operation, in May, it had about 40 Yorks, 40 Dakotas and 14 Hastings engaged in the operation. Cost to the British taxpayer in money was approximately £8,600,000 up to mid-June 1949. The real cost was eighteen men killed in five fatal accidents. On balance, a great victory had been won by Major-General William H. Tunner, U.S.A.F., commander of the Combined Air Lift Task Force (and former O.C. of the wartime India-China operation over the Himalayan "Hump"), and his second-in-command, Air Cdre. J. W. F. Merer, A.O.C. No. 46 Group, R.A.F. Higher Command over the Task Force was shared by Air Marshal Sir Arthur Sanders, succeeded in November 1948 by Air Marshal T. M. Williams, and their American opposite number, Lieut.-General John K. Cannon. These are names to rank with the great leaders of two World Wars.

Chapter Three

Firedog sets a New Pattern

Not a single problem of the class struggle has ever been solved in history except by violence.

Lenin. *Report to the Third All-Russian Congress of Soviets. January 24th, 1918.*

OPERATION PLAINFARE had been a cold war struggle against the spread of Communism. Elsewhere in the world, and particularly in south-east Asia, this doctrine was to take on a more aggressive character. However, it became all too easy to look for a Russian bogey behind every disagreeable situation, without making any attempt to distinguish between various forms of Communism or even to suspect that a different "ism" entirely might lie at the root of the trouble, such as blind nationalism.

Seeing how readily the British had been prepared to leave India in 1947, and how a campaign of murdering forces sent to maintain peace and order had helped to establish the independent state of Israel in the former Holy Land in 1948, dissidents in many countries prepared to get rid of their colonial leaders. They were encouraged by the great Communist powers, who realised that such a process would spread achievement of their worldwide aims without direct involvement, and by the well-intentioned but muddled thinking of U.S. politics which tended to cut its own throat and that of its friends.

Malaya served as the prototype for countless "hot war" situations that were to make the first quarter-century after World War II peaceful only insofar that it did not bring World War III.

The sole effective local opposition to the Japanese in Malaya had come from Communist guerrilla forces, mainly Chinese. VJ-Day, in August 1945, had left them well armed and unwilling to return to a pre-war system of control, under a British high

27

commissioner. Accordingly, they began a series of attacks on property, and atrocities against civilians who were allegedly pro-British, that were to initiate the longest continuous campaign by armed forces from the U.K. since the Napoleonic Wars.

Key base for the R.A.F. was Kuala Lumpur, which originally had been converted for use by the local flying club from an old tin-mining site two miles south of the federal Malayan capital city of the same name. It had been used briefly by the R.A.F. in 1941, but was still no more than a grass strip with basha buildings when the air force returned in 1948, at the start of the "Firedog" emergency air campaign against the terrorists. By the time the operations ended, it was to grow into a modern military air base, extending over 132 acres of land and with buildings valued at £1,200,000.

First units to arrive at Kuala Lumpur on July 1st, 1948, were No. 60 Squadron with Spitfire F.R.XVIII's – which was to be the last R.A.F. squadron to use this famous type as a fighter – No. 28 Squadron, also with Spitfire F.R.XVIII's, No. 110 Squadron with Dakotas, a contingent of the R.A.F. Regiment, and Base Depot Staff of the R.A.F. Regiment (Malaya), together with a communications squadron and a station flight. No. 45 (FB) Squadron, with Beaufighters, followed in August.

Under an overall reduction of British forces in the Far East in mid-1947, when the area seemed to have become calm, Nos.28 and 60 had each had their wartime complement of sixteen aircraft halved by the Far East Air Force Command. Simultaneously, garrison troops for the whole of Malaya and Singapore were reduced to the 1st Battalion Seaforth Highlanders, the 1st Battalion The Devonshire Regiment and a few Gurkha companies. When a State of Emergency was declared in May 1948 (a month before the start of the Berlin airlift) the Seaforths moved up-country to Kluang, and, with the R.A.F., waited for things to happen. It was not a long wait.

As reports of terrorist attacks on rubber plantations came in, the Spitfires set out to find and photograph the gangs responsible. From a height of 16,000–18,000 ft., it seemed like looking for the proverbial needle in a haystack, as nothing can disappear more rapidly and thoroughly than a handful of guerrillas in a jungle. Quite frequently, however, the enemy camps could be picked out on the recce photographs, and then a strike was mounted at once. The height at which the reconnaissance had been flown now became an asset. Confident that they could not have been located from such an altitude, the terrorists often did not bother to move camp quickly. The first intimation that they were no longer safely hidden came when cannon and machine-gun fire from low-flying "Spits" raked their camp, seemingly from all sides at once.

In a variation of this technique, troops were sometimes called in to beat an area of jungle, in the hope that the terrorists would make for the *lalang*, areas of tall grassland, where the Spitfires were waiting, guns and rockets ready.

Such strikes achieved little obvious effect. Even when some of the Communists were killed, their colleagues usually managed to remove the bodies and all traces of a successful action. Only the knowledge that they were keeping the enemy on the run, making him apprehensive each time he heard an aero-engine, and so having an effect on his morale offered any reward to the pilots and ground staff, working long hours in the tropical heat.

Back in England by this time, front-line squadrons were flying Meteor and Vampire jet-fighters. Single aircraft of each type had been sent to Singapore for tropical trials; but when the time came for the Kuala Lumpur squadrons to re-equip, and be reinforced, the new arrivals were still piston-engined. No. 45 Squadron exchanged its Beaufighters for Brigands in 1950. Even when it next re-equipped, it had to make do with Hornets. Fine aircraft, with a top speed of 472 m.p.h., fixed armament of four 20-mm guns and underwing racks for 2,000 lb. of bombs or rockets, they were nevertheless the last piston-engined fighters in first-line service with the R.A.F. anywhere. They were finally superseded by Vampire jet fighter-bombers in June 1955.

The first Vampires in the Far East had gone to No. 60 Squadron, at Tengah, Singapore, in December 1950; and in due course this unit received the faster Venom F.B. Mk. 1, which carried the same weapon load as the old Hornet but did so at speeds up to 640 m.p.h. Many other types of aircraft contributed to "Firedog". In fact, a final tally compiled by the Far East Air Force in 1960 listed no fewer than 31 different basic types, in 36 versions. It contains some surprises. For example, it is often forgotten now that the big Sunderland flying-boats of Nos. 88, 205 and 209 Squadrons made 958 sorties to attack the terrorists, each carrying 200 fragmentation bombs.

Equally surprising is the discovery that little Auster "spotter" 'planes of No. 656 Squadron far surpassed the record of any other type, by flying a total of 13,973,300 miles in 145,495 sorties, plus another 3,500,000 miles flown under Army command in 1957–60. Valetta and Dakota transports amassed the next biggest totals of flying hours, followed by Lincoln four-engined bombers and Whirlwind helicopters. Such a variety of types emphasises the complex nature of "Firedog".

As the campaign developed, it became a long drawn-out war of attrition. The land forces relied almost entirely on air support when in the jungle to engage and harry the enemy, whose technique was to strike quickly, murdering, robbing and blackmailing those they regarded as unfriendly, setting fire to homes and then melting away into the jungle.

The larger transport aircraft – which meant mainly Dakotas, and Valettas from 1950 – parachuted their loads weekly, daily and sometimes hourly into remote dropping zones, under hazardous flying conditions, in support of small forward parties of troops and police hunting the elusive enemy. Light transports, like the STOL (short take-off and landing) Pioneer, and helicopters flew into and out of tiny landing zones and airstrips to support patrols and forces manning jungle forts, to evacuate casualties and to ferry in and out troops, tracker dogs and supplies.

Strikes by Kuala Lumpur's fighter squadrons were supplemented with massive attacks by R.A.F. Lincoln heavy bombers from March 1950, when No. 97 Squadron, based at Waddington, became the first of several units detached to Tengah for operations against terrorists in Negri Sembilan. They were joined by the Australian-built Lincoln Mk. 30's of No. 1 Squadron of the Royal Australian Air Force from 1950 to 1958. In that period, No. 1 dropped over 33 million pounds of bombs and flew more than two million miles. Most of the time, its bombs just disappeared into the jungle and the crews turned for home, hoping it had all been worthwhile. One of the few occasions on which their hopes were confirmed was on May 13th, 1957, when a notorious Communist leader known as "Ten Foot Long" and four of his followers were killed in a raid near Seremban.

These Lincolns were by no means the only non-R.A.F. aircraft engaged in "Firedog". British Army pilots flew the Austers, and Royal Navy Whirlwind helicopters clocked some 600,000 miles in short hops in and out of the jungle in 1953–56. Vampires and Venoms of No. 14 Squadron of the Royal New Zealand Air Force flew 630 strikes in 1955–58; and the Canberra jet bombers of No. 2 R.A.A.F. and No. 75 R.N.Z.A.F. Squadrons flew a total of 50,000 miles on sorties from Tengah in 1958–59. The R.A.A.F. dropped millions of pounds of supplies from its Dakotas and Bristol Freighters, and introduced a new technique into this strange war in 1959 when it moved the supersonic Sabres of Nos. 3 and 77 Squadrons into its base at Butterworth. Only 68 sorties were flown in two strikes by the Sabres. During one of these operations, the sonic booms created by the aircraft as they dived over a jungle hamlet where terrorists were hiding were sufficient by themselves to flush out the enemy, who ran straight into a waiting ambush.

It is easy to overlook the work done on the ground by a further arm of the air force – the R.A.F. Regiment – yet, in some respects, the results it achieved were easier to measure. Six of its squadrons, numbered 91 to 96, took part in the security forces' ground operations in the jungle, with up to five tours of duty each. In many fierce engagements, they were credited with a total of about 19 terrorists killed, 57 wounded or captured and some 300 enemy camps and dumps destroyed. Of the 13 medals and awards, and 64 Mentions in Despatches they earned, none called for more courage than the two Military Medals gained by members of No. 94 Squadron in 1951. In an action at Bukit Munchong, five terrorists were killed, but only at the cost of five airmen killed and eight others wounded.

By comparison, the war fought from the air was strange, almost uncanny, in that the enemy was hardly ever seen or even known to be in areas of jungle blasted with guns and bombs, or showered with propaganda leaflets.

Looking back now, it may seem that the most valuable and enduring work was done by the helicopters and the Pioneer aircraft of No. 209 Squadron, which learned how to fly into landing areas so small that the longest was little more than 200 yards in extent, hacked out of living jungle and situated in winding valleys or on steep hillsides where turbulent air and bad weather were almost normal. At least this taught important lessons on the kinds of go-anywhere aircraft that were needed to fight the new kind of war.

When the R.A.F. set up its original Casualty Evacuation Flight with Dragonfly aircraft at Seletar, Singapore, in April 1950, this was the first time it had ever tried to use helicopters operationally in a combat area. The Flight quickly proved its worth and was expanded into the R.A.F.'s first helicopter squadron, No. 194, on February 1st, 1953. Operating from Changi, Singapore, and later Sembawang, the Dragonflies could each carry two casualties in stretcher panniers on each side of the cabin. They also carried voice-broadcasting equipment to appeal to the terrorists to surrender, and spraygear to spread destructive chemicals over the terrorists' crops.

First hint of the future "gunship" role of the helicopter was probably given in 1951. After an ambush, the driver of the vehicle concerned was airlifted back to the scene in a "chopper", accompanied by a soldier with a Bren gun. They caught the terrorists unawares and gave them a taste of their own medicine from the air.

Passengers included prisoners who were whisked out of the jungle in 10 to 20 minutes, instead of the usual four to five days, for interrogation by intelligence experts. In 1951, also, a complete Aborigine settlement in northern Malaya was evacuated after operations by paratroops of No. 22 Special Air Service Regiment, many being flown out by helicopter and liking the experience far more than travelling by motor car. Helicopters played an important part in setting up the jungle forts at this time. One of the main objects was to offer protection, medical care and education to the Aborigines, who were re-settled round the forts to break the terrorists' control over them.

By the end of November 1954, the Dragonflies had completed nearly 6,000 sorties, during which they evacuated 675 casualties from the jungle and airlifted more than 4,000 passengers, plus 84,000 lb. of supplies. This was pretty impressive for such a small machine; but long before the Dragonfly was withdrawn from Malaya in June 1956, the Royal Navy had begun to demonstrate what could be done with the larger Sikorsky S-55 Whirlwind.

In their very first operation on February 16th, 1953, three S-55's put down troops around a house that was being used as a terrorist HQ, near Port Swettenham. While a 194 Squadron Dragonfly hovered overhead, covering the attack with a Bren gun, the soldiers moved in and captured the building. Soon after this, No. 194 was itself re-equipped with Bristol Sycamores, with which it flew some 34,000 sorties from Kuala Lumpur in four years up to the end of 1958. No. 155 Squadron flew 45,500 sorties in Whirlwinds from the same base in this period. Then, in 1958, the two squadrons were amalgamated to form No. 110, with both types of "chopper". This unit was still in action when the Emergency was officially stated to be over on July 31st, 1960, with 8,000 operational sorties to its credit.

"Firedog" had cost the R.A.F. a total of 76 men killed and 4 wounded.

The end of such a campaign is as strange as the campaign itself. No great army was defeated in the field, and everyone seemed to carry on with their work as if nothing had really happened. It had even seemed likely at one time that the Emergency would end as early as 1955. Knowing that Malaya's chief minister, Tungku Abdul Rahman, would soon be going to London to discuss the granting of self government, with full independence within the Commonwealth likely to follow in August 1957, the Communist leaders felt that they might gain more by accepting a projected amnesty and returning to civilian life than from further fighting. They could hardly claim any longer to represent the people after elections in which an 80 per cent poll had given victory to the moderate Alliance party in 51 out of 52 constituencies. In any case, worldwide Communism was preaching a new policy of co-existence which made the Malayan conflict seem absurd.

In a meeting with the Tungku near the Thai border, Chin Peng, secretary of the Malayan Communist party, promised that his men would lay down their arms as soon as responsibility for internal security was transferred from the British to the federal government. Unfortunately, he could not agree that former terrorists should stay in detention until they had proved their loyalty as citizens. So, in the end, Chin Peng went back into the jungle and the amnesty offer to an estimated 2,600 remaining terrorists was withdrawn in February 1956. By that time, the fight had cost the federation alone over £120 million.

British and other Commonwealth forces stayed in the new federation of Malaya after independence and some are still there as this book is being written, as a key part of the nation's defence. Theirs has been no simple "watch and wait" assignment, for after Sarawak and Sabah had been added, to produce Malaysia, Indonesia began to assert its claims over these territories in Borneo, and for two and a half years the R.A.F. was in the forefront of the "confrontation" with this new power in south-east Asia. But, by then, it too possessed new strike weapons of unprecedented, frightening capability.

c

AIRCRAFT TYPES, HOURS, SORTIES AND MILES FLOWN
BY FEAF IN "FIREDOG" EMERGENCY

	Hours	Sorties	Air miles
Anson, 1948–54	2,028	1,365	202,800
Auster, 1948–60*	139,733	145,495	13,973,300
Beaufighter, 1948–50	1,935	1,347	290,300
Beverley, 1958	3	2	350
Brigand, 1949–52	7,780	4,513	1,322,600
Bristol Freighter, 1955–60	2,783	883	389,600
Buckmaster, 1950–52	40	50	6,400
Canberra B2, 1955–60	388	225	186,000
Canberra B6, 1955–56	749	408	359,500
Canberra PR7, 1955–56	52	20	25,000
Chipmunk, 1960	8	6	1,000
Dakota, 1949–60	32,542	16,263	3,905,000
Devon, 1949–55	1,465	1,444	190,500
Dragonfly, 1950–56	5,360	7,676	321,600
Harvard, 1948–56	2,352	1,845	258,700
Hastings, 1954–57	79	46	15,800
Hornet, 1951–55	7,827	5,625	1,722,000
Lincoln, 1950–58	18,137	5,576	3,264,700
Meteor PR10, 1954–60	7,758	4,584	3,491,100
Mosquito (PR), 1948–55	12,806	5,007	2,433,100
Mosquito (FB), 1951–55	153	148	29,100
Pembroke, 1954–59	1,967	1,859	275,400
Pioneer, 1953–60	16,766	28,512	1,676,500
Twin Pioneer, 1960	94	69	10,300
Sabre, 1959–60	110	68	52,800
Spitfire (PR), 1948–54	2,678	1,880	803,400
Spitfire (FB), 1948–51	3,838	3,530	1,155,400
Sunderland, 1948–58	5,656	958	678,700
Sycamore, 1953–60	14,936	35,850	896,200
Tempest, 1949–51	2,849	2,357	925,900
Valetta, 1950–60	37,875	20,466	5,681,250
Vampire, 1951–56	1,691	2,256	710,200
Venom, 1955–58	1,039	1,145	477,900
Whirlwind H.A.R.4, 1954–60	18,140	51,643	1,088,400
Whirlwind (RN), 1953–56	9,799	22,800	587,900
York, 1954	27	25	4,700
	361,443	375,849	47,413,350

* Austers of 656 AOP Sdn, when under Army command (1958–60), flew another 45,000 hours or 3,500,000 miles. In the same period it is estimated that other Army Auster units detached for Firedog operations flew some further 20,000 hours, or 1,720,000 miles.

Chapter
Four

Per Ardua

The revolutionary people constitute more than nine-tenths of the world population . . . Anybody can see for himself who in the end will be master of the world.

Mao Tse-tung, June 1960

When "Firedog" ended, more or less successfully, it had occupied the Royal Air Force for nearly one-third of the life of the service. But much more had happened in those years between 1948 and 1960. In a sense they had seen the R.A.F. building up to its all-time peak – not numerically, for the thousand-bomber raids and huge fighter sweeps of World War II were things of the past – but in sheer strike power and efficiency. They had also seen the beginning of political miscalculations and muddled thinking that were to throw away what had been created by the brilliance of Britain's aircraft industry and the courage of its air forces, so that in the end the newspapers were to write, with some justification, of an "air marshals' revolt".

As year succeeded dreary year, the R.A.F. struggled on with obsolescent equipment and inadequate funds. This was 1919 all over again. Older members of the service must have thought back to Lord Trenchard's famous *White Paper*, published in that year. Once again there was need to recreate an "air force spirit" and to lay the foundations for a castle in an era when ministers wanted only cottages. And, as in 1919, those in command were wise enough to recognise the truth of Trenchard's reference to "that on which the whole future of the Royal Air Force depends, namely the training of its officers and men."

One early hope was not fulfilled. In the spring of 1946, the wartime Empire Central Flying School was renamed Empire Flying School and charged with providing a centre for co-ordination and discussion of training matters, in conjunction with the reborn Central Flying

School and its counterparts in the Dominions. In the event, it was the C.F.S. which resumed eventually its old status as the worldwide spiritual leader in flying training.

Reformed at Little Rissington in Gloucestershire on May 7th, 1946, the C.F.S. became once more a training centre for flying instructors. Just as it got nicely under way, Britain was hit by a bout of winter weather of a severity unknown since the early months of 1940. Flying was impossible, so members of No. 98 Course, which had started on the first day of 1947, were sent home on indefinite leave. When conditions improved they were recalled, only to become so completely snowed-in that food had to be dropped to them from transport aircraft at one stage.

Cut off from the outside world, except by telephone, the more adventurous spirits decided to dig their way through to the village of Stow on the Wold. This plan was shelved when one of the officers, already up to his ears in snow, struck something metallic with his spade and discovered that it was the *top* of a "Halt at Major Road Ahead" sign. Operation Shovel was then switched to the shorter route leading to the Old New Inn at Bourton-on-the-Water.

Course 98, which should have lasted twelve weeks, was completed in twenty-six. It showed that the period allocated for instructor training would be too short, even in good weather, and soon pilots were spending 18 weeks, and then 24 weeks at Little Rissington before qualifying for the coveted initials "c.f.s." after their names.

The aircraft they flew at first would have seemed quite familiar to war-trained pilots. In mid-1948, for example, the C.F.S. possessed 17 Tiger Moths, 34 Harvards, 10 Mosquitos, seven Lancasters and four Spitfires, plus three single-seat Vampires to provide jet experience. This was hardly the kind of equipment one would expect at the premier training centre of the nation that had produced the first successful jet-engine more than a decade earlier; but it reflected the vintage nature of so much of what the R.A.F. still flew.

Nothing made this more apparent than the one and only attempt to resurrect the pre-war R.A.F. Display, at Farnborough, on two days in July 1950. Nearly 200,000 people flocked to the airfield in good weather to see what was voted the best-ever show of its kind. Afterwards, *The Aeroplane* told in glowing terms of the excellence of opening attractions that included massed bands, gliding displays, a mortar attack by a detachment of the R.A.F. Regiment, a demonstration of the work of R.A.F. police dogs and "musical jerks" by a bevy of attractive W.R.A.F. girls; but it was forced to admit that some youngsters viewed these items with a jaundiced eye and the comment:

"Let's get on wiv' the flying; we get ruddy P.T. at school every day!"

The R.A.F. did its best. Vampires fired rockets into a pair of dug-in "enemy tanks". Defending Meteors chased away Hornets and Mosquitos that simulated an attack on the airfield. No. 263 Squadron put on a fine show of formation aerobatics in their Meteor 4's. Hoverfly 2 helicopters, disguised as pink "heliphants" complete with trunks and ears, performed a circus act under the direction of a sartorially perfect ringmaster, complete with red coat, white breeches, a topper, a fearsome moustache and an enormous whip. Mosquitos of Nos. 14 and 98 Squadrons reconstructed the famous wartime attack on Amiens prison, escorted by Spitfires of Nos. 610, 611 and 613 Squadrons, and harassed by Spitfires of Nos. 5 and 17 Squadrons masquerading as Messerschmitt Bf 109s. The whole show ended with a massed fly-past by 225 aircraft of the R.A.F., U.S.A.F., R.C.A.F., R.A.A.F., S.A.A.F., R.N.Z.A.F., R.I.A.F. and R.P.A.F., supported by French Vampires and Belgian Meteors.

Star of the show was Pilot I. Posta of No. 17 Anti-Aircraft Co-operation Squadron, who performed spectacular aerobatics in a Spitfire XVI. All of the fighters were of basically wartime design; all of the bombers, flying-boats and transport aircraft were piston-engined. But two events in 1950 were to bring about great changes.

The Berlin Airlift had achieved far more than simply keeping alive half of an ex-enemy city. It had convinced the western powers that Russian ambitions would be held in check only by a permanent display of *united* military power and alertness. In June 1949 a squadron of Dutch Meteors had flown to the U.K. to take part in a British air exercise. Another large-scale British exercise, three months later, drew in combat aircraft from Belgium, France and the Netherlands, as well as U.K.-based B-29 and B-50 Superfortress bombers of the U.S.A.F.

The North Atlantic Treaty Organisation (NATO) had come into existence on August 24th that year, as a "security league" involving Belgium, Canada, Denmark, France, Iceland, Italy, Luxembourg, the Netherlands, Norway, Portugal, the U.K. and the U.S.A. Greece and Turkey were to be added in 1951 and West Germany in 1954. Meanwhile, NATO began to become effective following a decision by its Council in December 1950 to establish an integrated force for the defence of Western Europe under a Supreme Headquarters Allied Powers, Europe (SHAPE) and with the mutually respected wartime "supremo", General Dwight Eisenhower, as the first Supreme Allied Commander Europe (SACEUR).

The British Air Forces of Occupation, Germany, led by Air Vice-Marshal Sir Harry Broadhurst, formed the basis of the 2nd Allied Tactical Air Force, with responsibility for close support of NATO troops throughout Northern Europe and for assisting in the defence of the entire area against air or ground attack.

This positive reaction to "cold war" tactics was matched by America's response to an even more ominous "hot war" move in the Far East. On June 25th, 1950, North Korean troops swept across the 38th parallel into South Korea. On the initiative of the U.S.A., the United Nations Security Council met immediately to discuss the threat. A resolution was passed two days later recommending that members of the United Nations should furnish such assistance to the Republic of Korea as was deemed necessary to repel the armed attack and restore international peace and security in the area.

U.N. forces were placed under the overall command of General Douglas MacArthur, victor of the Pacific War against Japan. He had a difficult task. Exploiting the advantage of complete tactical surprise, the North Koreans took control of all but a small corner of the peninsula, around the port of Pusan, by mid-September. Supported by fighters and bombers based in Japan, the U.N. forces then counter-attacked and by November 2nd had pushed back, well past the 38th Parallel, almost eliminating the Northern armies. It was at this stage that elements of eleven Chinese Communist divisions entered the war and began a bitter struggle that was to last until July 27th, 1953, when a truce was finally signed.

The Royal Air Force played only a small part in the Korean War. From mid-September 1950, British troop reinforcements were flown out by Transport Command, and Auster A.O.P. flights, with Army pilots, served with distinction. R.A.F. pilots helped the R.A.A.F. squadron in Japan to convert from Mustangs to Meteors, prior to its participation in the air fighting; others flew with U.S.A.F. combat units to gain experience in jet-age tactics. And, once again, the veteran Sunderland flying-boats displayed their versatility, by becoming the only R.A.F. aircraft to see operational service in the war.

It was not the first time that No. 88 Squadron had clashed with the Far East brand of Communism. Based at Kai Tak, Hong Kong, one of its Sunderlands had taken a doctor and medical supplies to the Royal Navy frigate *Amethyst* when it was cut off and under shell-fire from Chinese batteries along the Yangtse river in April 1949. A second machine was so heavily damaged by enemy fire, near the ship, that it barely managed to limp to Shanghai. In the following month,

three Sunderlands of No. 88 evacuated 121 British civilians from that
city to Hong Kong.

When the Korean War began, No. 88 immediately organised
reconnaissance cover for Royal Navy ships blockading the enemy
coastline and began a ferry service between Iwakuni in Japan and
South Korea. It was joined in August 1950 by No. 209 Squadron,
fresh from its "Firedog" operations in Malaya; and by September the
Sunderlands were hunting for submarines and mines as far north as
Vladivostock. Even after both squadrons had been transferred to
Malaya in June 1951, a small detachment stayed at Iwakuni to
maintain patrols around the Korean coastline.

Far more significant than this direct involvement was the effect
that the Korean War, and the build-up of NATO forces in Europe,
had on the re-equipment of the Royal Air Force. Mercifully, the
assumptions that Britain would not become involved in a major
war for several years, and that Russia would not have an atomic bomb
until at least the early 'fifties had been justified; but the service was
at a dangerously low ebb as the new decade opened.

Britain's aircraft industry had not been idle. In the years since
World War II, it had produced an endless stream of prototypes and
design studies, both to officially-issued specifications and as private
ventures. Aircraft demonstrated at the R.A.F. Display in 1950 had
included a prototype English Electric Canberra, a twin-engined jet
bomber which – like the wartime Mosquito – was so fast and
manoeuvrable that it needed no defensive armament to escape interception by enemy fighters. Both Supermarine and Hawker had
new swept-wing single-seat fighters under development, each capable
of exceeding the speed of sound in a dive and, like the Canberra,
powered by Rolls-Royce's superb new Avon turbojet engine.

Much more hush-hush was the generation of warplanes that had
been taking shape for years in the experimental 'shops of the traditional British bomber companies.

Back in 1936, these same companies had begun work on machines
like the Stirling, Halifax and Manchester/Lancaster family that were
to spearhead Bomber Command's great wartime offensive. Now, a
decade later, they were able to plan aircraft so much more formidable
that they seemed likely to make any future major war unthinkable.
For the aircraft themselves, the designers were able to take advantage
of German research into swept-wing aerodynamics and utilise the
unrivalled power of turbojets from Rolls-Royce and Bristol Siddeley.
Behind the scenes, the British scientists who had contributed so
much to the perfection of America's atomic bombs were evolving

improved weapons that could be carried by these aircraft.

This combination of highly-advanced aircraft and nuclear weapons, plus electronic countermeasures devices able to incapacitate any radar search equipment and anti-aircraft missile guidance systems in use on the other side of the Iron Curtain, was to give the R.A.F. its V-bomber force.

As originally planned, Shorts were to produce an interim "straight"-wing design to Specification B.14/46. Known as the Sperrin, this four-jet bomber may have appeared conventional and unadventurous, but it was a formidable strike weapon by any standards. Ability to deliver a 10,000-lb. bomb-load over a range of 3,860 miles was coupled with a top speed of 564 m.p.h. and an over-the-target ceiling of 42,000 ft. The optimum nuclear bombers which Avro and Handley Page were contracted to develop, to Specification B.35/46, were to be far more advanced, with delta and crescent wing planforms respectively.

To Shorts' dismay, a fourth contender for production orders came on the scene in 1948, when Vickers proposed a swept-wing four-jet bomber with a performance between that of their B.14/46 and the two B.35/46 projects. This was so attractive and comparatively easy to build that the Sperrin was never again regarded as anything but a research aircraft, and the Air Ministry drafted Specification B.9/48 around the Vickers design.

So, at the start of the Korean War, prototypes of a whole range of very advanced new British swept-wing and delta-wing fighters and bombers were under construction, still without any obvious intention by the government of ordering any of them into large-scale production. To fill some of the gaps in an air force that was such a key unit of NATO's shield and striking force, America offered to supply B-29 Superfortress bombers under its military aid programme. So, in 1950, this famous aircraft, which had dropped the first atomic bombs on Japan in 1945, became the first U.S. type to enter service with the R.A.F. since the war. No. 149 was the first of eight Bomber Command squadrons to use the aircraft, which was given the name Washington B.1. A total of 88 were delivered eventually and did much to convince R.A.F. aircrews of the advantages of roomy pressurised cabins by comparison with the cramped and rather noisy accommodation on the Lincoln. It was no coincidence that Bomber Command's most coveted award, the Lawrence Minot Trophy for bombing efficiency, was won by Washingtons of Nos. 90 and 115 Squadrons in 1952 and 1953 respectively.

Next U.S. type to bolster the depleted Royal Air Force was the

Lockheed Neptune maritime reconnaissance aircraft, deliveries of which began in January 1952. More than 50 were operated by four Coastal Command squadrons until 1956-57, by which time there were sufficient Avro Shackletons to replace them.

Fighter Command and the 2nd T.A.F. were likewise given a transfusion of interim transatlantic equipment in 1953-56, when about 430 Canadian-built F-86E Sabre Mk.2 and Mk.4 jet fighters were put into service pending the arrival of British swept-wing designs. The aircraft were flown across the Atlantic by No. 1 Long Range Ferry Unit of Transport Command (later No. 147 Squadron) under Operation Bechers Brook, and Nos 3, 67 and 71 Squadrons of the 2nd T.A.F. became the first R.A.F. units to fly swept-wing fighters in May 1953.

It was an opportune move, for relations between East and West had continued to deteriorate and the R.A.F. was badly in need of an aircraft with the reputation of the Sabre, which had established a marked superiority over the Russian-built MiG-15 in Korea. But, at last, the British government had realised the folly of making do any longer with World War II veterans and hand-outs from America, and the Royal Air Force was about to enjoy, for an all-too-brief period, the knowledge that it was equipped with aircraft second-to-none in the world, all designed and built in Britain.

The first move was made on January 29th, 1951, when Mr Attlee, the Prime Minister, announced plans to speed up rearmament of the British services. They included call-up of the 20 Royal Auxiliary Air Force fighter squadrons, for three months of refresher training with Fighter Command. Nine of these squadrons were equipped with Vampires and six with Meteors. The other five still flew Spitfires, as did the 1,000 Volunteer Reserve pilots who were also called up for three months.

The R.A.F. estimates for that year rose to £328,750,000, the highest since the war, and it was estimated that front-line strength was 50 per cent higher than in 1948, although there were little more than 250,000 officers and men in the service. Next year the estimates were again increased, to £467,640,000, much of it allocated to expansion of the 2nd T.A.F. in Germany.

By this time the R.A.F. was equipping with its first jet bomber, the Canberra, which had entered service with No. 101 Squadron at Binbrook in May 1951. An outstanding success from the start, this great aircraft was destined to remain in first-line service for twenty years and to be built in the U.S.A. and Australia because even the U.S. industry could produce nothing so good.

Nor could the government ignore any longer the urgent need for new fighters and heavy bombers. The prototype of Sydney Camm's Hawker Hunter did not fly until July 20th, 1951; but by that time production was already gathering momentum under an initial order for 113 received by the company in October of the previous year. As an insurance against failure of the Hunter, two prototypes and 100 production examples of the Swift were ordered from Supermarine in the following month. These became the first swept-wing fighters of British design to enter service, with No. 56 Squadron, in February 1954; but, ironically, it was the Swift that ran into such severe control problems that it was eventually abandoned as an interceptor, while the Hunter became one of the truly great fighters of the 'fifties and 'sixties.

As a first, rather grudging step towards the projected V-force, the Vickers B.9/48 Valiant bomber was ordered into production in April 1951. By June of the following year, the international situation was so bad that no further delay in ordering the more advanced Avro Vulcan and Handley Page Victor was conceivable, and contracts were placed for both types. Indeed, the possibility of war was by then so real that the government instituted a "super-priority" programme, under which types like the Hunter, Swift, Valiant, Victor, Vulcan and the new Gloster Javelin twin-jet two-seat all-weather interceptor were assured of preference in the supply of raw materials and equipment needed to get them into operational service as quickly as possible.

To ensure the high quality of aircrew needed to fly these new types, the R.A.F. had revised its entire training technique. With typical boldness, it first decided to switch from traditional slow, low-powered *ab initio* trainers like the old Tiger Moth and Prentice, and the newer Chipmunk, to the 550-h.p., 200-m.p.h. Hunting Percival Provost. There was no shortage of critics eager to predict the death and disaster that would result from doubling the power of the aircraft on which pupils began their flying training. However the superb manoeuvrability of the Provost, coupled with the fact that pupil and instructor sat side-by-side, produced an immediate improvement in the quality of pupils passing from basic to advanced training, whilst setting new standards of safety.

By 1953, the old Prentice/Harvard sequence had given way to a new scheme under which all pupils began on Provosts and passed on to two-seat Vampire T.11s before going to an operational conversion unit for final training on front-line types. Encouraged by the success of this venture into high powers, Hunting Aircraft suggested that the next logical step was to replace the Provost by a jet basic trainer, so that pupils would handle nothing but jets throughout their time at Flying Training Schools. The idea seemed to make sense for an air force that was rapidly converting to jet power in all its combat squadrons; but the idea of putting a pupil in the cockpit of an aircraft as fast as a Battle of Britain Hurricane fighter from his very first lesson appalled some people.

To satisfy their own curiosity and silence the critics, the Air Ministry ordered from Hunting nine Jet Provosts, with the same basic airframe as the piston-engined variety but powered by a Viper turbojet and fitted with a retractable undercarriage. In August 1955, two courses of pupils at No. 2 Flying Training School, Hullavington, were started side-by-side on piston-engined and Jet Provosts respectively. On October 17th, Pilot Officer R. T. Foster soloed on a Jet Provost after only 8 hours 20 minutes dual instruction. Despite the complications of high power and speed, advanced instrumentation and radio, and retractable undercarriage, others followed quickly and it was decided eventually, in 1957, that the Jet Provost would become standard basic equipment in Flying Training Command, making the R.A.F. the first service in the world to adopt an all-jet training sequence.

The cost of this expansion and re-equipment was high. R.A.F. estimates increased year by year, to £498 million in 1953, £537 in 1954 and £621 million in 1955, including considerable sums provided by the U.S.A. under its military aid programme. There was, however, no doubt of the quality of the aircraft which the money was buying. Even the least knowledgeable members of the public could appreciate this when an R.A.F. Canberra flown by Flt. Lt. R. L. E. Burton and Flt. Lt. D. H. Gannon won the speed section of the London-New Zealand air race in October 1953, covering the 12,270-mile course in under 24 hours; and when a Hunter, not so very different from production models, raised the world speed record to 727.6 m.p.h. on September 7th of the same year.

It was also encouraging to note that the 640 aircraft which flew past Her Majesty Queen Elizabeth II on the occasion of her Coronation Review at Odiham, on July 15th, 1953, included 440 jets. Even these cold statistics tell only half the story, for among the aircraft were the first prototype Victor, the second prototype Valiant, the first prototype Vulcan, the third prototype Javelin, the first production Hunter and a flight of Swifts. Allied to the knowledge that the first British atomic bomb test had already been conducted successfully in the Monte Bello Islands, off Western Australia, on October 3rd, 1952, this gave more than a hint of the growing strength and capability of the service.

Unfortunately, it was just as obvious that the R.A.F.'s commitments were likely to increase in a world where the prophets of Communism, nationalism and anti-colonialism were preaching subversion and revolution. It was nothing new for the service to have to cope simultaneously with several trouble-spots. So, whilst keeping up its offensive against terrorists in Malaya, it waged a whole succession of other campaigns as Empire crumbled into Commonwealth.

Typical was the part it played in suppressing the Mau Mau rebellion in Kenya, which began in October 1952. Members of the Mau Mau, a Kikuyu secret society, were obsessed with the belief that their tribe should possess more of the land. So they stirred up a wave of violence and terrorism against European settlers, the government and any of their own people who refused to support them. Army units in the country were reinforced, but lacked any form of air support.

Among those most conscious of the deficiency were R.A.F. instructors based at training schools in Southern Rhodesia. The aircraft they flew were Harvards, and they knew that similar machines had been used with tremendous success by U.S.A.F. pilots in Korea, to find, and mark with smoke bombs and rockets, targets for United Nations fighters and bombers. If the slow old Harvard could do that kind of work in a real war, there seemed no reason why it should not be equally useful for tracking down and attacking the elusive Mau Mau gangs in Kenya . . . it was at least worth a try.

So, in March 1953, No. 1340 Flight was formed at Marrian's Farm, Nyeri, under Squadron Leader Jack Trant. With a strength of four Harvards, four pilots and 25 ground crew, it turned itself into a light attack unit, by mounting a Browning machine-gun, with several hundred rounds of ammunition, in the starboard wing of each aircraft and hanging under the wings racks for eight 20-lb. anti-personnel bombs. Co-operating with ground forces and with Piper Pacer lightplanes of the Kenya Police Air Wing, which marked targets with phosphorous flares, the Flight soon achieved such success in hunting the Mau Mau that it was allowed to expand to nine aircraft and ten pilots.

In its first ten weeks of operations, it flew 183 offensive sorties and attacked 85 targets with a total of 1,100 bombs and 69,000 rounds of ammunition. In doing so, it left little doubt of the part that air power could play in demoralising the terrorists and helping the army to round them up. So, although the Harvards continued to play a key role throughout the four years of the emergency, they were backed up periodically by more orthodox combat types.

Typical were the operations flown by seven Lincolns of No. 49 Squadron in the Autumn of 1953. Whilst on a training exercise in the Middle East, they were diverted to Kenya to help deal with a reported concentration of ten Mau Mau gangs near the Harvards' base. In one subsequent action, two Lincolns, nine Harvards and every available police spotter-plane swept over the thick forest areas where the terrorists were hidden. Nearly ten tons of high explosive were dropped and many thousand rounds of ammunition fired. British troops of the 39th Brigade, waiting on the edge of the bombing line, then went in to mop up stragglers.

Other squadrons which helped to force the Mau Mau out of their forest hide-outs into the open in this way were No. 61 with Lincolns, detached from the U.K., and No. 8, with ground attack Vampire 9s, from Aden. By September 1955, the security forces had accounted for 14,000 terrorists and a great many were undergoing rehabilitation. Nine months later, the troubles were virtually over.

The part that the Lincoln, last of the R.A.F.'s piston-engined heavy bombers, played in operations like those in Malaya and Kenya is often overlooked. In a jet age it did a difficult task superbly; but its familiar, noisy piston-engines, bristling gun turrets and narrow, unpressurised crew cabins were relics of World War II and in January 1955 the first of the R.A.F.'s new jet V-bombers, the Valiant, entered service with No. 138 Squadron at Gaydon. In the following month, it was announced that Britain would proceed with the development and production of hydrogen bombs to be carried by the new generation of aircraft. The U.S. and Soviet air forces had already demonstrated the possession of such weapons and were planning new means of delivery by intercontinental missiles. Clearly the world was getting a very dangerous place in which to live.

Nobody doubted in this era that the future, or lack of future, of Britain, and civilisation as a whole, now rested in the hands of air power. The deterrent policy of "peace through fear" was building up to a peak of frightening efficiency, and land, sea and air forces were becoming more and more inter-dependent. There seemed little doubt that one day they might even be integrated, and it was significant that when the post of Chairman of the Chiefs of Staff

Committee was created in Britain on October 25th, 1955, the first holder of the title was Marshal of the Royal Air Force Sir William Dickson. It was a good choice, for he had gained immense experience of combined operations on the North-West Frontier of India in the 'thirties and as Commander of the Desert Air Force in 1944–45, and had, in fact, started his service career in the Royal Naval Air Service before the creation of the R.A.F.

Most of all, the appointment of an air force officer as "supremo" of the country's armed forces must have given pleasure to the architect of Britain's air power, Lord Trenchard, in the last months before he died, on February 10th, 1956. Seldom had one man's dream been so richly fulfilled in his lifetime.

This was in many respects the year in which the R.A.F. attained its highest peak of reputation and morale. Its strength was only beginning to grow, and in the fifth year of a Conservative government that had succeeded the penny-pinching post-war era of Socialism, there seemed no reason to doubt that Britain would continue to wield its influence as a world power far into the future, under the protection of its nuclear shield. It was an illusion soon to disappear in the wake of two consecutive political onslaughts.

First was a consequence of the Suez campaign in 1956. The eight-year-old state of Israel had been threatened with extermination by its vastly stronger Arab neighbours, headed by Egypt which was receiving massive military aid from the Soviet Union and Czecho-slovakia. To forestall the expected invasion, Israeli forces had begun operations in the Sinai Peninsula at nightfall on October 29th.

Britain and France were in a difficult position. It was the refusal of the western powers to supply further arms to the Arab countries, in the hope of reducing tension in the Middle East, that had caused Egypt to turn to the Communist *bloc* for aid. In retaliation, the U.S.A. and Britain had withdrawn their financial support for the Aswan High Dam project that was so vital to the improvement of living standards in Egypt. President Nasser responded in turn by announcing on July 26th, 1956, his intention to nationalise the Suez Canal, in which Britain and France were the major shareholders, in order to raise funds for the dam. The two western powers at once began concentrating powerful naval forces in the Mediterranean and air forces in Malta and Cyprus to protect their property and people in the Canal Zone.

At the time of Israel's offensive, therefore, the R.A.F. had the Valiants of Nos. 138, 148, 207 and 214 Squadrons, Canberras of 9, 12, 15, 101, 109 and 139 Squadrons, and Shackletons of 37 Squadron at Luqa and Hal Far, Malta; Hunters of Nos. 1 and 34 Squadrons, Canberras of 10, 15, 18, 27, 35, 44, 61 and 115 Squadrons, and six squadrons of Hastings and Valetta transports at Nicosia, Cyprus; and Venoms of 6, 32, 73 and 249 Squadrons, Meteor NF.13 all-weather fighters of 39 Squadron, reconnaissance Canberra PR.7s of 13 Squadron, Valiant reconnaissance-bombers of 543 Squadron and Austers of 1903 Flight at Akrotiri, Cyprus. The Royal Navy carriers *Eagle, Albion, Bulwark, Theseus* and *Ocean* were in the area, with powerful complements of strike aircraft, fighter-bombers and helicopters, as were the French carriers *Arromanches* and *Lafayette*. And seven squadrons of French fighter-bomber, reconnaissance and transport aircraft were based in Cyprus and Israel.

Fearful that the Israeli attack might make matters worse in the Canal Zone, Britain and France delivered an ultimatum to both sides on October 30th, calling upon them to end the fighting and stay clear of an area ten miles on each side of the Canal. Failing the acceptance of these conditions, it was implied that the two nations would implement Operation Musketeer, under which British and French troops would be landed from the sea to occupy key points along the Canal.

Israel accepted the terms, but Egypt refused. So, the fighting continued and the British and French fleets set sail for Egypt, covered by the Shackletons from Luqa and, later, R.A.F. Hunters and French Thunderstreaks from Cyprus.

After warning the Egyptians of their intentions, via Cairo radio, to reduce civilian casualties, Valiants of 148 Squadron and Canberras of 10 and 12 Squadrons made heavy attacks with 500 lb. and 1,000 lb. bombs, from high altitude, on eight of the nine airfields in the Canal Zone and four more in the Nile Delta. Far from using its MiGs to break up these raids, the Egyptian Air Force evacuated many of them, and its Il-28 jet bombers, to apparent safety in Syria and far-away Luxor. It was a wasted effort, as the 20 Il-28s at Luxor were put out of action a few days later by French Thunderstreak fighter-bombers.

The R.A.F. attacks were continued on the nights of November 1st/2nd and 2nd/3rd. Reconnaissance photographs showed that many Egyptian aircraft had escaped the initial bombing, so subsequent raids were made at lower altitude. Hunter escorts were also dispensed with, as there was so little opposition and it was felt that the fighters could do a better job providing cover for the approaching naval forces.

Strike aircraft from Akrotiri and the carrier task forces ranged freely over the target area in daylight, and by November 3rd the Egyptian Air Force had virtually ceased to exist. About 260 of its aircraft had been destroyed, including most of the 120 MiGs and 50 Il-28s that were in service when the campaign began. Only eight of them had been lost in air combat.

Having eliminated the opposing air force, the French and British squadrons switched their attacks to tank concentrations and supply depots, to clear a path for the troop landings scheduled for November 5th. In the early hours of that day a force of more than 750 paratroops were dropped from the six Cyprus-based squadrons of Hastings and Valettas on Gamil airfield and from French Noratlases and C-47s south of Port Said. Close support was provided by carrier-based aircraft, and a smaller French air-drop was made at Port Fuad later in the day.

By the morning of the 6th, all immediate objectives had been seized and landings of men, vehicles and supplies from the sea began at dawn. Marine Commandos were ferried ashore by Whirlwind helicopters of 845 (Naval) Squadron and the Joint Experimental Helicopter Unit, which then instituted a casualty evacuation service. The Israelis, meanwhile, had conquered the entire Sinai Peninsula, except for a narrow strip along the Canal which they did not occupy. In doing so, they lost only 171 men killed, against 3,000 Egyptians killed and 5,850 captured, together with 30 Soviet tanks, 100 armoured vehicles, 1,000 trucks and the Egyptian destroyer *Ibrahim-el-Awal*.

This is not the place to discuss the political justification of the Suez operation, or even if Britain and France were more aggressive in trying to regain the Canal than were the Russians who put down the Hungarian uprising at the same time with little more than a "tut tut" from the United Nations. The significant fact is that, under pressure from the U.N. and under threats of all-out military intervention by the Soviet Union, Britain and France agreed to a cease-fire which came into force at midnight on the 6th. The Suez Canal was lost to them for all time and the future would show the ineffectiveness of the so-called U.N. peace-keeping force which was to be sent to maintain stability in the Middle East.

For the first time, Britain had been compelled by other nations to retreat from what had seemed to her leaders a position of right and honour. The defeat was political, not military; but it made many people begin to question whether the United Kingdom had any future as a world power. Was this ridiculous at a time when the Royal Air Force was building towards the target of being able to destroy the world's mightiest military machine virtually single-handed? The answer seemed to come in the government *White Paper* on Defence published under the authority of Minister of Defence Duncan Sandys in April 1957.

The official comment that it foreshadowed the greatest change in a defence system ever made in normal times was no overstatement. It was some relief to know that work on the R.A.F.'s first true supersonic fighter was to continue, but in other respects the government had clearly been brain-washed into believing that manned aircraft were becoming outdated and would soon give way completely to missiles for both attack and defence.

Two quotes from the *White Paper* are sufficient now to show how utterly misguided it was. Dealing first with defence against attack, it stated: "In view of the good progress already made (with surface-to-air missiles), the government has come to the conclusion that the R.A.F. is unlikely to have a requirement for fighter aircraft of types more advanced than the supersonic P.1 (Lightning), and work on such projects will stop." The views expressed on offensive aircraft were summed up in the paragraph: "Having regard to the high performance and potentialities of the Vulcan and Victor medium bombers and the likely progress of ballistic rockets and missile defence, the government has decided not to go on with the development of a supersonic manned bomber, which could not be brought into service in much under ten years."

So began a thirteen-year period of wrong decisions, indecision and muddled thinking, under successive governments, that was to reduce the Royal Air Force from one of the greatest powers for peace that the world had ever known to a service that was probably smaller than the German and Swedish air forces in terms of numbers of first-line combat aircraft. Well might one recall the words of David's lament over Saul and Jonathan: "How are the mighty fallen, and the weapons of war perished!"

D

Chapter Five

Ad Astra?

Britain's influence in the world depends first and foremost on the health of her internal economy and the success of her export trade. Without these, military power cannot in the long run be supported. It is therefore in the true interests of defence that the claims of military expenditure should be considered in conjunction with the need to maintain the country's financial and economic strength.

White Paper on Defence: "Outline of Future Policy"; April 1957

For nearly a year after publication of the Sandys *White Paper* on Defence the Air Ministry maintained an official silence concerning the contents. Did this mean that the leaders of the Royal Air Force were satisfied with the "Outline of Future Policy"? The answer came, dramatically, on May 6th, 1958, when the Air Ministry pioneered a new concept of closer understanding between the services and public by inviting representatives from a wide cross-section of the national life to its Conference Prospect, in the Royal Empire Society's Assembly Hall in London. Among those present was the Queen's consort, H.R.H. Prince Philip, Duke of Edinburgh, already noted for his outspoken views and himself a fine pilot who had trained with the R.A.F.

Next morning, some London newspapers viewed Prospect as "the air marshals' revolt" against Duncan Sandys and his policies. In fact, it was nothing of the kind. The hall was not filled with the sound of grinding axes and nobody glossed over the need to equate weapons with what Britain could afford financially. This would have been a waste of time at the end of a five-year period in which defence absorbed an average 10 per cent of the country's gross national product; when 7 per cent of its entire working population was either in the services or supporting them; when one-eighth of the output of the metal-using industries, so vital to the export trade, was devoted to defence; and when an unjustified proportion of the nation's top scientists and engineers were engaged in defence work.

The two basic facts of life then, as now, were that survival depended on maintaining a viable deterrent, to preserve the delicate military "balance" between east and west; and that this had to be achieved at an economical cost that would not ruin the nation economically. Where the government and the R.A.F. differed markedly was in the way in which these two conflicting factors might be reconciled most effectively. Thus, Prospect took the form of illustrated talks and playlets which outlined problems relating to the operation, equipment, training and manning of the R.A.F., including the impact of new weapons, and suggested how the problems should be met.

The opening remarks were by Marshal of the Royal Air Force Sir Dermot Boyle, first Chief of the Air Staff to have graduated from the service's own college at Cranwell. He explained that the Conference had been called: "Because there has been, and still is, great confusion in many people's minds about the role of the Royal Air Force. . .We feel that this confusion is bad for the country and for the service, and since we are quite clear in our minds what our responsibilities are and how we are going to meet them, we feel that nothing but good can come from telling you what we think. . . "

It is a pity that the Defence Minister, who had accepted an invitation to attend, was not there. Many subsequent huge and costly mistakes might have been averted. In the event, Prospect proved to be a breath of sanity and clear thinking that wafted briefly over the military scene, appearing to promise a more stable policy but having no real chance of success in a period dominated by the theories of financial wizards and phoney scientists.

Air Commodore F. E. Rosier, Director of Plans at the Air Ministry, set out clearly the R.A.F.'s commitments as: "Firstly to maintain the deterrent; secondly to contribute to the shield force in NATO; thirdly to contribute our quota to the Baghdad Pact and for the defence of South-East Asia; fourthly to provide the forces necessary for imperial policing." These have not changed up to the present day.

Over and over again it was emphasised that the basic policy behind all R.A.F. thinking was to prevent a war, not to fight it. If anyone in the U.K. had any illusions about his chance of survival in a nuclear war, they could be resolved by the knowledge that Bomber Command did not rely on making more than one all-out attack on the enemy before losing its home bases and organisation. On the other hand, the certainty of what that one raid could achieve was the strongest possible deterrent to any aggressor.

As Air Vice-Marshal W. H. Kyle, Assistant Chief of Air Staff

(Operational Requirements) commented: "It is worth reminding ourselves that these aircraft (the Valiants, Victors and Vulcans) have a performance superior to any other bombers in service in the world, certainly when it comes to penetrating enemy defences." He added that each could carry Britain's H-bomb, equivalent to one million tons of T.N.T., and it was a sobering thought that all the destruction rained on Europe by the Americans and ourselves in World War II was caused by just two million tons of bombs.

As for the possibility that the V-force might be destroyed on the ground, the A.O.C.-in-C. Bomber Command, Air Chief Marshal Sir Harry Broadhurst, said that his squadrons were planned to operate from dispersed bases under much the same system as Fighter Command, and could be organised to react to radar reports almost as quickly as their engines could be started. The Group Captain, Plans, Bomber Command, Group Captain D.C. Stapleton, told of the Avro rocket-powered H-bomb missile (Blue Steel) which was being evolved for the Mk.2 versions of the Vulcan and Victor and "by virtue of its relatively small size and very high speed will present the Russians with a tremendous interception problem. . . It will have its own guidance devices which will enable it to find and hit its target with great accuracy, regardless of weather conditions."

This was the time when good-intentioned but short-sighted people were campaigning to "ban the bomb"; but what was the alternative? As Air Cdre Rosier explained: "If we adopted any other strategy, if we supported renunciation of the nuclear weapon, or if we thought we should provide all possible measures against conventional attack on the grounds that the nuclear deterrent would never be invoked and that the war would be fought to its utmost by conventional means . . . we would be bound to ask for at least 1,000 bombers and at least 1,000 fighters, for tactical air forces on the scale of the last war and for a Coastal Command many times greater than the present force." This at a time when the government planned to end the call-up of National Servicemen and reduce the total strength of all three services from 690,000 to 375,000 persons within five years, of whom 140,000 would be in the R.A.F.

The government had implied that ballistic missiles like the big 2,000/2,500-mile-range Blue Streak, which de Havilland were developing, would supersede manned strategic bombers. It became clear during Prospect that the Air Ministry regarded the two types of weapons as complementary. While we could mount two different kinds of thermonuclear attack, our potential enemies would have to continue to prepare against both, to develop successive new and improved countermeasures, absorbing time, money, effort and manpower.

Air Vice-Marshal Kyle went so far as to say: "I suggest that we shall need what will amount to a second generation of these manned and unmanned weapons, and that they will continue to be complementary. This is not to say that we will cling to the idea that we need a bigger and better bomber as we know it now. That would be a reversal of decisions already taken and is not our intention. However, a manned vehicle, that is something retaining discretion, not tied to large and vulnerable airfields but still capable of delivering a weapon from outside an enemy's perimeter defences; and a ballistic missile capable of being deployed and launched without the inflexible fixed ground organisation now required, may be the answer."

This persuaded some newspapers to proclaim next morning that the R.A.F. was planning to carry the manned deterrent into outer space – which seemed a very literal and currently appropriate interpretation of the service's motto *Per Ardua ad Astra* (Through difficulties to the stars)!

Whatever Air Vice-Marshal Kyle intended by these remarks, he left little doubt that conventional manned combat aircraft would continue to be essential for many tasks, despite what Mr Sandys might think. Confirming reports that the R.A.F. was seeking a replacement for the Canberra, he remarked: "This will have to operate against modern and well-organised defences and act as a sanction against the outbreak of local aggression or as a means of preventing its expansion. For reasons of economy in development and in operational effort, it is essential that this aircraft has the greatest possible flexibility. It must combine very high performance with the ability to operate from restricted airfields. We must exploit the latest developments in navigation, bombing and reconnaissance equipment to give it an all-embracing capability as a strike/reconnaissance aircraft in all weather conditions. Bearing in mind that it will be in service during the 1965-70 era, we intend to combine to the full an aircraft of high speed at low altitude with a supersonic capability at high altitude."

This was the requirement that was to produce in due course the BAC TSR.2, still perhaps the most formidable multi-purpose combat aircraft conceived anywhere in the world.

As with bombers, so with fighters. In contrast to the expressed views of Mr Sandys, the Air Commodore, Operations, Fighter Command, Air Commodore P.G. Wykeham, was constrained to state: "We must soon give serious thought to a possible successor to the P.I (Lightning)." Explaining why, he said: "Fighters are a very flexible force that you can move around and concentrate just as you want to; and of course they can operate at much greater distances than we can ever hope to fire (surface-to-air) missiles. This would be of particular importance if the Russians developed a powered bomb which could be launched a long way from our coast. Another thing, fighters are the only means of dealing with aircraft which otherwise might fly up and down outside the range of our missile defences and jam all our radars... We can also use fighters to reinforce overseas."

There was much more to Conference Prospect. It emphasised that Transport Command would need a complete range of new strategic and tactical aircraft if it was to meet its commitments, and that replacements would be needed for the Whirlwind and Sycamore helicopters, the Twin Pioneer transport, and the older types serving Coastal and Flying Training Commands. It revealed interesting little sidelights, such as the fact that the R.A.F. would pay about £23 million to the Exchequer for fuel tax in 1958. Most of all, it emphasised how far the reality of what the services really needed had diverged from the dream-world of the professional politicians and their pre-occupation with financing more popular projects like the welfare state. For that reason alone, no apology is made for reporting Prospect at such length. If its views had been regarded, Britain's defences would have been infinitely stronger in the 'seventies and countless millions of pounds would not have been thrown away without so much as a nut and bolt to show for them.

The extent to which the government intended to regard the views of its military leaders was shown when the time came to order a large freighter to ferry Blue Streak missiles to Australia for testing at the Woomera range. There were four possibilities. The Army would have liked the R.A.F. to order a turboprop development of the ungainly but immensely versatile Blackburn Beverley; but this lacked the necessary range and speed. Nobody favoured the Britannic, a turboprop transport that Shorts proposed as a development of the Bristol Britannia airliner. The R.A.F. had been the first air force in the world to operate jet transports when it took over and modified Comet 2 jet-liners intended originally for B.O.A.C. and they had convinced it of the advantages of jet travel. For that reason it would have liked a version of the big four-jet VC10 that Vickers was designing for the airlines, but this was believed to be a little too big and "hot" to get into R.A.F. bases overseas. So, the R.A.F. had decided on a transport development of the Victor bomber.

When the contract was announced in Parliament, it appeared that the government had overruled the R.A.F. and decided to order the Britannic (later renamed Belfast), in order to provide some relief of the unemployment situation in Northern Ireland where Shorts have their factory.

The story of other military aircraft and missile programmes during the late 'fifties and 'sixties is so depressing and reads so much like an "Alice in Wonderland" fantasy that it seems almost unbelievable. However, it must be set out in some detail as it has governed the entire composition, capability and efficiency of the Royal Air Force to the present time.

In his 1957 *White Paper*, the Minister of Defence suggested that the Avro supersonic bomber, then under development, was to be abandoned because it could not be put into operation in much under ten years, by which time it would have been overtaken by missiles. In fact, at the end of the following ten years, the R.A.F. was having to soldier on with Vulcans and Victors because it had nothing newer to supersede them. What, then, had happened to all the ballistic rockets and missiles?

Back in 1958, it had seemed that Mr Sandys' plans might be bearing fruit when America supplied to Bomber Command 60 Thor intermediate-range ballistic missiles to supplement the V-bombers. They were not quite R.A.F. property, as their nuclear warheads remained under U.S. control and could not be armed for use without the personal O.K. of the American President. This did not matter for long, as they were on their way back across the Atlantic by 1963, as obsolete as the dodo.

The all-British Blue Streak, able to carry a far more powerful warhead over much longer ranges, should have been available by then. Unfortunately, it had become clear some years earlier that this missile also was too vulnerable to surprise attack to have much value as a deterrent, and it had been abandoned as a military rocket in April 1960, after £84 million had been spent on it.

It had been decided to utilise instead a different kind of ballistic missile – the American-designed, air-launched Skybolt which could be carried by the V-bombers. But the by-now-familiar pattern was soon repeated; in December 1962 Skybolt joined the military Blue Streak on the scrap-heap because the U.S.A.F. no longer wanted it and Britain considered that the cost of developing it alone would be too great. The cost this time to the British taxpayer was a mere £27 million, and two years of wasted effort.

Seldom has a worse decision been made. Only the protagonists of

the ballistic missile, as opposed to manned aircraft, salvaged anything from the Anglo-U.S. meeting that buried Skybolt, for in its
place Britain began planning for a force of four nuclear-powered
submarines, each to be equipped with 16 Polaris nuclear-armed
ballistic missiles. Before the last of these vessels has become operational, their usefulness is already beginning to seem doubtful. So,
with no replacement for the V-force ordered or contemplated, the
British nuclear deterrent that has always seemed so vital hardly
exists at the start of the 'seventies.

The picture might have seemed brighter had the one new combat
aircraft considered essential in 1957 – the Canberra replacement –
reached fruition; but this was cancelled by the Socialist government
of Harold Wilson in April 1965, after the prototype had been demonstrating for months its potential as the world's outstanding strike/
reconnaissance aircraft. At a time of financial stringency, only an
export order from Australia could have saved it. How fortunate it
was that the decision to order the Spitfire and Hurricane into
production in 1936 had not been dependent upon overseas sales.

To prevent the possibility of anyone resurrecting the TSR.2 at a
later date, existing airframes and jigs were ordered to be smashed to
pieces. It is difficult to appreciate how such behaviour could possibly
have encouraged the exports that were considered so all-important.
In fact, by 1966 Britain's aircraft industry had been so merged,
mutilated and messed about for years that it sold a total of fewer than
150 civil aircraft and helicopters to overseas customers that year.
In contrast, Boeing's sales of more than 400 jet-liners in a year included
53 Model 747 "jumbo-jets" which, by themselves, cost a total sum
nearly twice as great as the export earnings of the entire British
aircraft industry in 1966.

Time after time it has been proved that the best way of creating a
healthy home industry is by the revenue and experience gained from
military contracts, but the Prime Minister had also announced early
in 1965 cancellation of the Hawker Siddeley P.1154 supersonic
V/STOL (vertical/short take-off and landing) fighter in favour of
American Phantoms, and of the HS 681 STOL transport in favour
of the Hercules, also built in America. To save money and give the
British industry some share in the work, parts of these aircraft were
to be manufactured in the U.K., and the Phantoms were to be fitted
with Rolls-Royce engines and British electronics. In the event, this
not only added considerably to the ultimate cost of the Phantoms
but produced power plant problems that had to be solved before the
aircraft could display their full potential.

In place of the P.1154's it was decided to order 60 (later 77) single-seat P.1127 (Harrier) V/STOL close-support/reconnaissance aircraft for the R.A.F., plus 11 (later 13) similar two-seat operational trainers. Although of lower performance, these aircraft were to represent one of the few successes of all recent U.K. military aircraft programmes, as will be explained later.

Far less happy were attempts to find a lower-cost replacement for the TSR.2 and a successor for the V-bombers. To fill the first of these gaps, 50 F-111K tactical combat aircraft were ordered from America. On paper it looked a good move. The F-111K utilised a revolutionary "swing-wing" that enabled it to combine Mach 2.5 performance with good weapon-carrying capability and modest airfield requirements. Unfortunately, it never lived up to its promise. The airframe, and particularly the swing-wing, gave persistent trouble and aircraft delivered to the U.S.A.F. were grounded for long periods. Three of the first eight F-111's sent to reinforce American units in Vietnam were lost in a matter of weeks. Parliament was assured that even if the aircraft did not meet in full the requirements of the U.S. services it would still be good enough for Britain. Nevertheless, the contract *was* cancelled and again the R.A.F. got nothing for millions of pounds paid out in cancellation charges.

Then there was the equally sad story of the Anglo-French variable-geometry (swing-wing) aircraft that was intended to replace the V-bombers in the 1970s. It was a product of the new technique of cutting costs by sharing development and production with an overseas partner and Britain's Defence Minister, Denis Healey, had described it as "both operationally and industrially the core of our long-term aircraft programme". This time it was the French who decided, in June 1967, that they could not afford the programme and the aircraft progressed no further.

When an order for Boeing CH-47 Chinook heavy-lift helicopters for the R.A.F. was cancelled within weeks of being signed, the taxpayer had good reason to begin questioning what he had to show for a total of £35,000,000,000 spent on defence between 1946 and 1968/69 —an average of about £660 for every man, woman and child in the country.

In fact, the Royal Air Force had continued to meet efficiently and economically every demand made upon it while these unsettling events were happening. At the time the 1957 *White Paper* was being drafted, it had about 185 squadrons with 2,000 aircraft, of which about one-third were fighters and one-quarter bombers. The last Sabre squadrons had been re-equipped with Hunters in the Spring of 1956. A few months later, the last Lancaster was retired. The build-up of Transport Command continued, and three squadrons of Prestwick Pioneers were formed to support the new mobile Army brigade, with one each intended to be based in the U.K., the Middle East and the Far East.

Even more significant was the first air-drop of an operational atomic bomb from a 49 Squadron Valiant, in trials at Maralinga, Southern Australia, on October 11th, 1956 – an event which was followed quickly by the first test-drop of an H-bomb over Christmas Island from another aircraft of the same squadron, on May 15th, 1957. The deterrent was beginning to get very sharp teeth.

Reference has been made already to the part that Cyprus played as a base for the Suez campaign in 1956. As the Headquarters for the Middle East Air Force, it formed a vital link in the overseas command network; so it was particularly worrying when years of agitation by the Greek Cypriots, led by Archbishop Makarios, for *enosis* (union) with Greece flared up into a campaign of violence. The guerrilla bands of E.O.K.A. (the National Organisation of Cypriot Struggle), under Colonel Georgios Grivas, launched a series of terrorist attacks on British service personnel and establishments that were to continue for three years, until the Autumn of 1958.

As in Malaya, helicopters quickly proved their worth as military aircraft during this emergency. No. 284 Squadron began to receive British-designed Sycamore 14's in November 1956 and logged more than 8,000 hours with them in the following two years, during which it pioneered the techniques of night flying and of dropping troops to track down members of E.O.K.A. in mountainous terrain. In over 16,000 sorties, it dropped 3,271 troops in terrorist-frequented country and trained a further 13,000 in the art of scrambling down ropes from hovering helicopters. No. 284 also evacuated 222 casualties from hill and forest areas, including soldiers seriously wounded in E.O.K.A ambushes, dropped 113 tons of food, ammunition and stores to the security forces, and even fought forest fires.

This was one campaign in which the usual kinds of combat air-craft were of little use, and the most valuable types sent out from the U.K. to work alongside the Sycamores were Whirlwind helicopters, Chipmunk spotter-planes and Pioneer STOL transports. Theirs was a difficult, thankless task, and nobody was sorry when it ended in the Autumn of 1958, following the release of Archbishop Makarios from detention and the suggestion that Cyprus should become a republic after a period of self-government. Independence became reality in 1960, with Britain retaining sovereignty over only 99 square miles around the military bases of Dhekhelia and Akrotiri. The A.O.C.-in-C. Middle East Air Force was made responsible for administration of these sovereign base areas and the R.A.F. was thus secure in a key strategic position.

Not all the local, small-scale campaigns had such a happy ending. For years the R.A.F. battled against dissident tribesmen in its role as protector of Aden, Oman and the Trucial States. This was tough, dangerous work, calling for operation from dusty airfields, in a hot climate, and for attacks on a cunning enemy, hidden among rocks in craggy mountain areas. Ground attack Hunters proved especially adept in rocket attacks on the tribesmen's mountain strongholds, sometimes placing their weapons with great accuracy only 25 yards from the positions of British troops.

Many other types performed sterling service in operations from R.A.F. Khormaksar, Aden, not least the gargantuan Beverleys which tended to disappear in a cloud of dust when delivering or picking up troops of the Federal Regular Army from up-country rolled-sand airstrips.

Yet, in the end, Aden was evacuated, leaving the superb base facilities open for use by Russian-built MiG fighters in the insignia of the new South Yemen Republic and, presumably, any other Soviet aircraft that might care to operate in the area.

When Indonesia threatened the newly-formed Federation of Malaysia, by laying claim to Sabah and Sarawak, it was the R.A.F. which provided much of the defences, patrolling the Straits of Malacca to spot and intercept landing parties in small ships, dropping leaflets over places in Indonesia, and supporting the troops who had to counter raiding parties along 300 miles of mountains, swamps and jungle marking the border between Indonesia and Sarawak.

No. 225 Squadron alone flew more than 19,000 sorties in its Gnome-Whirlwind helicopters, carrying 40,000 passengers and 800 tons of freight in 4,000 flying hours during its first year of operations from Kuching, the capital of Sarawak. Among the passengers were more than 600 patients carried on ambulance flights—at least half of them local men, women and children in need of urgent medical attention, and expectant mothers. This type of operation *was* appreciated by the Malaysians, who sometimes decorated their long-houses with pictures of the Whirlwinds. One grateful mother even named her newly-born daughter "Helicopter" in recognition of the ambulance that had carried her to hospital.

Such assistance to the civilian population was by no means limited to Malaysia. It has been a traditional part of the service's duties wherever the R.A.F. has been based or has flown since the war. At home, the yellow-painted Whirlwind rescue helicopters are a familiar sight along our summer coasts, and hundreds of people are now alive and safe only because they were hauled from the sea as exhausted swimmers, from rubber dinghies drifting away from land, from rocks and cliffs cut off by the incoming tide or from ships being battered to pieces by heavy seas. The same helicopters, and trained mountain rescue teams, have saved the lives of many injured climbers.

When the Colonial Office and Directorate of Military Survey wanted a photographic survey of 112,000 square miles of Aden Colony and Protectorate, it was done by R.A.F. Meteors, Canberras and Valiants.

In July 1960 aircraft of Transport Command, the M.E.A.F. and from Aden were made available to the government of Ghana to airlift troops, police and stores between Accra and Leopoldville in support of United Nations peace-keeping moves in the Congo.

Africa was again in the news in the following year, with R.A.F. transport aircraft first dropping food to famine-stricken Kenyans in March and April and then returning on October 1st for Operation Tana Flood. Widespread flooding had cut off whole areas and more than six million pounds of food were dropped in Kenya and Somalia before the operation ended in January 1962.

In November it was British Honduras, on the other side of the globe, that needed aid in the wake of hurricane "Hattie". Under Operation Sky Help, supplies were first flown across the Atlantic to Kingston, Jamaica, from where Transport and Coastal Commands organised a shuttle service between Kingston and devastated Belize.

At home, a Belvedere helicopter was called in to place the 80-ft. spire on top of the new Coventry Cathedral on April 26th, 1962. Three years later, when Rhodesia made its unilateral declaration of independence, a Javelin squadron was sent to neighbouring Zambia as a precautionary defence measure and Transport Command began a massive airlift of fuel on behalf of that country, delivering some $3\frac{1}{2}$ million gallons before it was able to hand over the task to others.

These were typical of many similar operations, big and small, by which the Royal Air Force demonstrated repeatedly its new ability to help the civil authorities in peacetime, all over the world. Each task, as well as saving lives or providing a service in time of need, was also valuable training for the kind of work that might have to be performed in any future cold or hot war.

Periodically, there were more traditional jobs to be tackled, as when Iraq laid claim to the newly-independent sheikhdom of Kuwait in mid-1961. At the request of the ruler, the R.A.F. despatched Hunter ground attack fighters and transport aircraft to Kuwait. By July 6th, 7,000 troops and 720 tons of stores had been moved into the Persian Gulf area, as well as Canberra bombers; and a force of V-bombers was held in readiness on Malta. Only after the Arab League had agreed to recognise the new sheikhdom and provide protection for it were the British forces withdrawn in October.

There was a revolt in Brunei to be quelled in the last month of 1962, and an urgent call to fly troops and police to Anguilla in 1969, to restore law and order after this tiny West Indian Island had decided to secede from the associated state of St. Kitts-Nevis-Anguilla.

Whilst performing these multitudinous, vastly-differing tasks, the R.A.F. never neglected its primary duty of training, planning, re-equipping and re-shaping itself for its main function. As old bases had to be evacuated, it concentrated into a smaller number of strategically-situated areas. New staging posts were built, like the airfield on the tiny island of Gan in the Indian Ocean. Flight refuelling became a routine technique, both to enhance operational capability and to enable even thirsty jet fighters to hop across the globe between the widely-dispersed airfields still available.

The V-bomber force, armed with Blue Steel H-bomb missiles and capable of becoming airborne within four minutes during a period of alert, remained fully capable of providing the all-important deterrent through the 'sixties. To cope with the new demand for a high-mobile force able to stamp out local troubles speedily, No. 38 Group came into being in Transport Command on January 1st, 1960. Nothing like it had been seen before. In one compact, self-contained Group, under Air Vice-Marshal Wykeham, were squadrons of fixed-wing transports, helicopters and Hunter ground attack fighters, trained to operate in conjunction with any other combat aircraft of the R.A.F. and Royal Navy that might be to hand.

The public had an opportunity to see 38 Group in action at the 1964 S.B.A.C. Display at Farnborough, for the R.A.F. was by then a regular participant in Britain's then annual aviation "shop window".

The idea was to demonstrate how air power could be used to put down and support an assault party of troops in an enemy-held area. Low-level 'attacks' by eight 38 Group Hunters, four Canberras of the 2nd T.A.F., and eight Scimitars and eight Sea Vixens of the

Royal Navy first showed how the area would be softened-up, after which the fighters orbited at 3,000 ft. to give air cover to the approaching waves of transport aircraft.

To secure the landing zone, a wave of six R.A.F. Wessex helicopters landed and deployed 90 assault troops of the 2nd Battalion The Parachute Regiment. Nearby, six Navy Wessex put down another 90 men from No. 43 Royal Marine Commando and No. 95 Commando, Light Regiment, Royal Artillery. A further wave of 12 Wessex then followed up with underslung loads comprising six 106-mm. recoilless missile launchers and six 105-mm. pack howitzers to support the landing parties. In yet another wave, three Wessex displayed methods of deplaning troops without landing. From the first, six men were roped down from 20 ft. From the others, hovering at up to 200 ft. altitude, Commandos demonstrated abseiling—a controlled descent by rope which is especially suitable for operations in jungle areas where trees prevent helicopters from hovering nearer the ground.

Meanwhile, six Argosy transports had arrived with vehicles and trailers and 120 R.A.F. Regiment personnel to provide a defence force for the continued protection of the landing zones. As the Argosies left in a stream take-off, Twin Pioneer transports and helicopters were already bringing in supplies and evacuating "casualties". It was all make-believe; but not long afterwards, as already mentioned, aircraft of No. 38 Group, including No. 225 (Gnome-Whirlwind) Squadron, were in the front line of the confrontation with Indonesia, in Sarawak.

The emergence of the "38 Group concept" was just one of the ways in which Britain's services girded themselves to maintain and even improve their fighting ability despite the loss of overseas bases, and reduction in funds and manpower. There was no longer any possibility of defending the entire U.K. against attack in a major war, so Fighter Command, re-equipped with its new Mach 2 Lightning interceptors, armed with air-to-air missiles of unrivalled efficiency and backed up by Bloodhound surface-to-air missiles, concentrated on defence of the V-bomber bases. And gradually a new NATO strategy was formulated, under which any conflict in Europe, started probably by mistake or miscalculation, would be contained by the use of non-nuclear weapons for a few days, while the politicians of both sides contemplated the mutual suicide of letting the war escalate and, began attempts to resolve their differences over a table.

The biggest problem is to survive the opening minutes of such a situation, as the Arab Air Forces discovered during their war with

Israel in June 1967. That is why the V/STOL Harrier is such an important element of the R.A.F. in Germany. Needing no runways or base facilities, it can be dispersed and hidden, with weapons, supplies and fuel brought to it by road or helicopter. It can then take off, fly at high subsonic speed to attack enemy targets and again "disappear" into the landscape before its next sortie.

An ability to take off and land vertically by jet-lift demands such high power that the weapon load of the Harrier was small at first; but it has grown in step with increases in engine output and, in any case, the load increases considerably when (as is usually the case) some forward run is practicable at take-off. Suggestions that the Harrier's range was too short for it to be of much practical value were scotched when one of the first machines delivered to No. 1 Squadron won the westbound section of the *Daily Mail* transatlantic air race in May 1969, flying non-stop from London to New York with the assistance of in-flight refuelling by Victor tankers. Subsequently, aircraft of the same squadron have deployed several times to the Mediterranean for practice in overseas reinforcement and weapons firing.

No other air force in the world has in service an aircraft like the Harrier, although it has been ordered for the U.S. Marine Corps. The same is true of several of the other new R.A.F. aircraft. The Nimrod maritime patrol aircraft, for example, carries equipment far more advanced than that of any competitor, for the vital task of tracking down and destroying enemy naval vessels and submarines. And the "swing-wing" Multi-Role Combat Aircraft, under development in partnership with German and Italian companies, should go a long way towards filling the gap left by cancellation of the TSR.2 and F-111K when it enters service in the mid-seventies.

At the beginning of its second half-century, the R.A.F. is very different from its counterpart of even a few years ago. At the top, it is no longer controlled by its own Air Ministry. Since 1964, all three services have been under the direct, unified control of the Ministry of Defence. Even Fighter, Bomber, Coastal and Transport Commands are no more. In their place, the home-based Strike Command operates five remaining squadrons of Vulcan Mk.2 bombers, Victor tankers, Buccaneer low-level strike and maritime attack aircraft, Shackleton and Nimrod maritime patrol aircraft, Lightning and Phantom supersonic all-weather fighters, and Bloodhound ant-aircraft missiles.

Air Support Command has taken over the strategic and tactical transport aircraft, helicopters and smaller fixed-wing types of the former Transport Command, plus No. 38 Group which has replaced its Hunters with Harriers and Phantoms. Training Command utilises Chipmunk primary trainers, Jet Provost basic trainers, Gnat and Varsity advanced trainers, twin-jet Dominies and Varsities for navigation and aircrew training, and a variety of other types, including Sioux and Whirlwind helicopters. None of its old skill has disappeared with the passing years, and it provides the R.A.F.'s premier—unrivalled—aerobatic display team in the shape of the Red Arrows, whose Gnats are flown by instructors from the Central Flying School.

The four home commands are completed by Maintenance Command. Overseas, too, the structure of the service has been much simplified, with only the Near East Air Force (HQ Cyprus), Air Forces Gulf (Bahrain), the Far East Air Force (Changi) and R.A.F. Germany (2nd T.A.F.) as permanent commands. How permanent remains to be seen. The Socialist government had planned to withdraw all British forces from east of Suez; but the Conservative government of Edward Heath, which came into power in mid-1970, has said that it will retain some units in the Far East, in support of S.E.A.T.O. Similarly, the Socialist plan to scrap the Royal Navy's big carriers and disband its fixed-wing aircraft squadrons, leaving the R.A.F. responsible for all maritime operations, may be changed.

The future, therefore, remains as full of interest as the past. In 1970, as this volume is being written, the Royal Air Force is small and may even appear weak in comparison with the R.A.F. of the mid-sixties, in the heyday of the V-bomber force. It is not the first time that it has appeared thus, and many enemies have lived to regret their underestimation of its capabilities. Even in a so-called technological age, brains are still better than computers, and the men of the Royal Air Force—as well as all of us who depend so much upon them—can continue to feel as confident as Admiral Lord Nelson who, before the Battle of Trafalgar, commented: "We are few, but thank God we are of the right sort."

Heads we win . . . Mosquito VIs of No. 2 Group show their paces to the citizens of Copenhagen at a victory fly-past on July 4, 1945. The machines were flown by the same crews that took part in the famous low-level attack on the Gestapo headquarters in Copenhagen before Denmark's liberation.

. . . and tails you lose. Rows of Focke-Wulf 190 tails in a bomb-damaged assembly plant at Bremen at the end of the war.

E

Disarming the *Luftwaffe* was one of the tasks of the British Air Forces of Occupation. Shown is a collection of Focke-Wulf 190s—a type produced in larger numbers than Spitfires—and Ju 52/3ms.

Many captured *Luftwaffe* aircraft were exhibited to the British public after VE-Day. Shown here is a Messerschmitt 163 rocket fighter in Hyde Park in September 1945.

At Farnborough some of the captured machines, including this Messerschmitt 262 twin-jet fighter, were evaluated in the air by R.A.F. pilots. This work was often extremely hazardous and one pilot lost his life while testing a Heinkel 162.
[*Aeroplane*

Spitfires prepare to take off from North Weald for the first Battle of Britain Day fly-past over London on September 15, 1945. Nearest the camera is Grp. Capt. Douglas Bader in the cockpit of his "personal" aircraft.

Above: Hundreds of operational R.A.F. aircraft were put into temporary storage at the end of the war, and scenes like this 'sea' of Airspeed Horsa gliders at Netheravon were not uncommon.
[*I.W.M.*

Most of the surplus aircraft, however, quickly found their way to the melting pot—including these veteran Coastal Command Halifaxes seen at York in December 1945.
[*Philip Moyes*

First of Britain's postwar problems in the Far East was Indonesia. With the Japanese defeated, a nationalist movement clashed with rival factions and the R.A.F. and British troops had the job of restoring law and order. Here armourers prepare a Mosquito F.B.VI for a rocket attack on a radio station in December 1945.
[*I.W.M.*

Before 1945 was out the R.A.F. gave a convincing demonstration of the possibilities of jet propulsion—then still in its very early days—by raising the world speed record by nearly 30 per cent, to 606 m.p.h. with this Meteor F.IV of the High Speed Flight. The pilot was Grp. Capt. H. J. Wilson.

First helicopter used by the R.A.F. was the Sikorsky Hoverfly I (U.S.A.A.F. R-4) which entered service at the Helicopter Training School at Andover early in 1945, one example also being used by No. 529 Squadron. Here one of the Helicopter Training School's machines is seen being demonstrated at an air display at Hendon in September 1945.

[Aeroplane

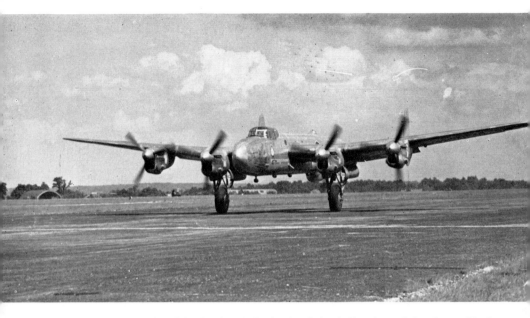

The famous Lancaster *Aries* of the Empire Air Navigation School, Shawbury, Salop, leaves Black-bushe airfield, Surrey, on August 21, 1946, on its record-breaking flight to Darwin, Australia.

In 1946—47 Lancasters of No. 15 Squadron joined with American Fortresses and Superfortresses in test bombing of German U-boat pens at Farge, near Bremen—Project *Ruby*. The Lancasters and Superfortresses dropped 22,000 lb. *Grand Slams*. Examples of the three types of bomber are seen at a Press facility at Bovingdon in May 1946.

Used for a short time in the immediate post-war period was the Short Seaford flying-boat, a development of the famous Sunderland. Eight Seafords were delivered to the R.A.F. (photo shows the last of them, serial number NJ207) and after serving briefly with No. 201 Squadron they were converted for civil use as Solents.　　　　　　　　　　　　　　　　　　　　　　[*Aeroplane*

Succeeding the Hoverfly I in R.A.F. service was the Hoverfly II (Sikorsky R-6A), 40 examples of which were delivered to Britain in 1946. The type was used for a while by the Airborne Forces Experimental Establishment and by No. 657 (A.O.P.) Squadron. One of the latter's machines is shown above, spotting for a battery of self-propelled 25-pounder Sexton guns at Larkhill, Salisbury Plain, in March 1948.

Airmen look over smoke bombs awaiting loading into Lancasters of No. 148 Squadron, Upwood, Hunts, standing by to make an 'attack' on the Fleet during exercise *Sunrise* in December 1948. By the end of 1949 Bomber Command's veteran Lancasters had been almost entirely supplanted by Lincolns.

Shades of *Target for Tonight*. Crew of an Avro Lincoln embark for a training sortie. The Lincoln—originally known as the Lancaster IV and V—was just too late to see action in World War II, but became the mainstay of the postwar Bomber Command until supplanted by Canberras and American-built Washingtons.

An early postwar transport aircraft of the R.A.F. was the Avro Lancastrian which entered service early in 1946. Within three years most had been sold to civil airlines or to aircraft manufacturers for engine experimental work.

Too late for operations with the *Tiger Force* against the Japanese in the Far East, the Hawker Tempest II saw postwar R.A.F. service both at home and overseas. From 1946 to 1948 the type formed a major part of the close-support ground attack component of B.A.F.O. in Germany and the picture shows aircraft of No. 33 Squadron which later (1949) moved from Germany to the Far East to become the only Tempest II unit to serve with F.E.A.F.

Left: Transport Command Dakota drops rations early in February 1947 to 1200 R.A.F. personnel, including W.A.A.F.'s, who had for days been snowbound and isolated at Binbrook airfield, Lincs.

Above: In 1948/49 the R.A.F. took part in the biggest air supply operation ever contemplated—the Berlin Air Lift, otherwise known as operation *Plainfare*. All told the R.A.F. made 49,733 flights, using Dakotas, Hastings and Yorks. Here, Yorks are shown parked in front of hangars at Gatow.

Below, left: Another mercy mission which involved R.A.F. Dakotas was the dropping of food supplies, in the summer of 1948, to the civil populace in large areas of India stricken by disastrous floods. Here sacks of grain or rice are kicked out of the door of a low flying 'Dak' over one of the flood-affected areas of Chittagong, Bengal.

Below: In the early days of the Berlin Air Lift, strenuous efforts were made to evacuate younger children from the city. Photo shows children being taken to a Sunderland of No. 201 Squadron waiting on Lake Havel to fly them to Hamburg in November 1948.

In order to augment the facilities of Tempelhof and Gatow in handling airlift supplies the Americans built a new airport at Tegel, in the French sector of Berlin. The airfield first came into use in November 1948 and among the first aircraft to arrive was this R.A.F. Dakota.

At the Empire Test Pilots School pilots of the R.A.F., Royal Navy and the Dominions air forces are taught the technique of testing modern aeroplanes. Seen here is a formation of some standard Service types flown by E.T.P.S. pilots in 1949—from foreground to background, D.H. Vampire V, Gloster Meteor IV, Avro Lincoln, D. H. Mosquito and a Fairey Firefly naval fighter.

[*Flight International*

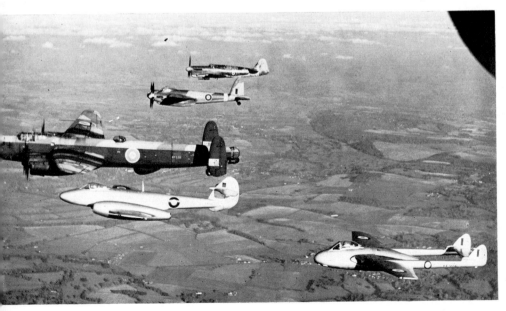

Groundcrews of Vampire F.B.5s of No. 26 Squadron, B.A.F.O., watch a General Aircraft Hamilcar tank-carrying glider landing at R.A.F. Gutersloh during an exercise in August 1949.   [*Aeroplane*

W.A.A.F. medical orderlies load a 'stretcher' casualty on to the external carriers of a Sikorsky Hoverfly II during a demonstration at R.A.F. Brize Norton, Oxford, in January 1949. The helicopters of this particular unit were maintained by R.A.F. personnel and flown by Army officers seconded to the R.A.F. unit for a period of two years.

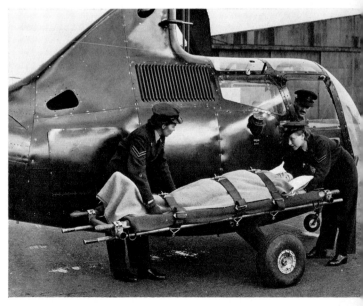

In 1949-50 two R.A.F. Auster 6s equipped to use floats, skis, or wheels, took part in the Norwegian-British-Swedish Antarctic Expedition. They operated during the landing operations on Queen Maud Land and afterwards surveyed hundreds of miles of coastline and hinterland.

Weekend airmen. *Opposite, top.* Aircrews of No. 501 'County of Gloucester' Squadron, R.Aux.A.F., make a practice 'scramble' to their waiting Vampires in 1949. This unit continued to fly Vampires up to the time that the auxiliary squadrons were disbanded, in 1957. *Opposite, bottom.* Ground staff of No. 613 'City of Manchester' Squadron, R.Aux.A.F., refuel their Spitfires during a visit to R.A.F. Horsham St. Faith, Norfolk, for an air display in March 1950.

Spitfires of Nos. 5 and 17 Squadrons, masquerading as Messerschmitt Bf 109s, fly to intercept the attacking Mosquitos in the set piece—a reconstruction of the famous World War II Amiens Jail raid—at the 1950 R.A.F. Display at Farnborough.   [Charles E. Brown

Firedog operations in the Malayan Emergency campaign of 1948-1960 involved 375,849 operational sorties, in the course of which 76 R.A.F. personnel lost their lives. Among the numerous types of aircraft employed on *Firedog* sorties was the Lincoln, detachments being sent from Britain to Tengah, Singapore, whence they made bombing raids on the jungle terrorists. (*Above*) Lincolns of No. 57 Squadron prepare for a strike from Tengah in 1950. (*Right*) Bombs fall from a Lincoln on to a suspected jungle hide.

de Havilland Vampire F.3s of No. 601 'County of London' Squadron, R.Aux.A.F. (*left*) and Gloster Meteor F.IVs of No. 263 Squadron R.A.F. (*above*), practise formation aerobatics for the R.A.F. Display which was held at Farnborough in July 1950. [*Charles E. Brown*

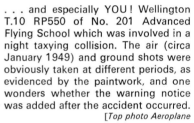

. . . and especially YOU! Wellington T.10 RP550 of No. 201 Advanced Flying School which was involved in a night taxying collision. The air (circa January 1949) and ground shots were obviously taken at different periods, as evidenced by the paintwork, and one wonders whether the warning notice was added after the accident occurred.

[*Top photo Aeroplane*

Handley Page Hastings of Transport Command arrives at an airfield somewhere in the Far East in October 1950 during the reinforcement of British forces in Korea. The Hastings superseded the Avro York as the R.A.F.'s standard long-range transport and its active career in squadron service extended from the time of the Berlin Air Lift until early 1968.

First British jet bomber and the first to serve with the R.A.F. was the English Electric Canberra which was chosen to supersede Lincolns and to form new squadrons of Bomber Command. First Service version was the B.2 and the first squadron equipped—in 1951—was No. 101 based at Binbrook, Lincs.

Above. Mosquito B.35 of No. 98 Squadron, R.A.F. Celle, Germany, pictured during the Western Union exercise *Cupola* in August 1950.

Lord Trenchard climbs into the rear cockpit of a Meteor T.7 before a local flight from Hucclecote with Polish-born Gloster test pilot Sqn. Ldr. Zurakowski (standing behind him) on October 12, 1950. Trenchard, always remembered as the 'Father of the R.A.F.', retained his keen interest in everything concerning the Service right up to the time of his death early in 1956.

Vampires abroad. Vampire F.B.5s of No. 6 Squadron, Middle East Air Force, stir up the desert dust at R.A.F. Mafraq, Jordan, during an exercise in 1950. The rudder of the nearest aircraft sports No. 6's famous winged can-opener insignia which first appeared on its tank-busting Hurricanes in World War II. (*Left*) Vampire F.B.5s simulating 'enemy bombers' are serviced at their base at Fassberg, Germany, during Exercise *Ombrelle* in June 1951. The black bands on the wings and tail were used to distinguish 'enemy' aircraft. In Germany the Vampire F.B.5 supplanted the Mosquito F.B.6 as the standard close-support aircraft and also equipped new squadrons, eventually becoming the backbone of the 2nd Tactical Air Force.

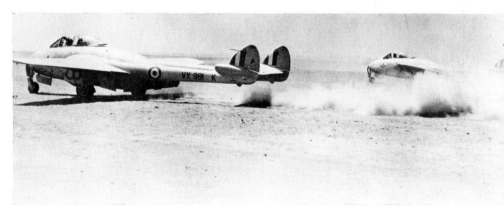

Fastest and most graceful twin piston-engined fighter to serve in the R.A.F. was the de Havilland Hornet which entered service in 1946. These examples, photographed in January 1951, are Mk.3s of No. 41 Squadron, Church Fenton, Yorks.   [*Aeroplane*

Armoured car of the R.A.F. Regiment on patrol among the hills in Iraq early in 1951.

Supplied to the R.A.F. under the American defence aid programme in the early 1950s were a number of Boeing B-29 Superfortresses which the R.A.F. named "Washingtons". Eight squadrons of Bomber Command used the type and some Washingtons were also operated in an electronic countermeasures role by No. 152 Squadron, Signals Command, one of whose aircraft is seen here.

Sir Hugh Lloyd, C-in-C Bomber Command from 1950 until 1953, chats with armourers preparing to bomb-up a Washington of No. 115 Squadron, Marham, during an air exercise early in 1951. Sir Hugh, who is seen wearing the badge of No. 9 Squadron which he commanded in 1938-39, coined the once well-known saying "The bomber is a rapier, not a bludgeon."

First British-built, albeit not British-designed, helicopter to enter R.A.F. service was the Westland-built Sikorsky S-51, known to the R.A.F. as the Dragonfly. Here an early example takes off from a clearing in the Malayan jungle in the early 1950s with a single externally-carried casualty.

Meteor F.8 sporting a nose probe and the blue and yellow chequerboard markings of 245 Squadron, Horsham St. Faith, refuels from a U.S.A.F. Boeing KC-29 tanker during experimental trials in 1951. From 1950 until 1955, when the Hawker Hunter became firmly established in squadron service, the Meteor F.8 was the major type of single-seat day interceptor with R.A.F. Fighter Command.

Line-up of Hastings transports at Nicosia, Cyprus, on November 1, 1951, during the 'round-the-clock' airlift of the 16th Independent Parachute Brigade to the Suez Canal Zone to reinforce the British garrison there, following Egypt's abrogation of the 1936 treaty. Other troops were flown to Suez from the United Kingdom during the crisis.

Most outstanding of postwar Short Sunderland operations was their contribution to the British North Greenland Expedition of 1951-54. Aircraft of
Nos. 201 and 230 Squadrons, operating during the few weeks of late summer
when the Greenland lakes were free of ice, carried several hundred tons of
equipment and supplies from Young Sound on the north east coast of Greenland to the expedition's base camp at Britannia Lake, some 800 miles from
the North Pole.

Men of the R.A.F. Regi-
ment learn how to strip
and reassemble a light
machine gun. Formed in
World War II, the R.A.F.
Regiment is responsible
for the local defence of
R.A.F. bases.

"Last night the tempera-
ture on the Air Ministry
roof was . . ." A picture,
taken in Whitehall, which
will undoubtedly be of
interest to everyone who
has ever wondered what
the B.B.C's weather men
were referring to!

No. 82 Squadron of Bomber Command was equipped with a special photographic reconnaissance Lancaster, the P.R.1, after the war and completed a
remarkable aerial survey of East, Central and West Africa, covering nearly $1\frac{1}{4}$
million square miles, between 1946 and October 1952. One of its aircraft,
PA427, which was retired in December 1953, was the last operational Lancaster in Bomber Command. Picture shows one of the squadron's aircraft at
Kabrik, Egypt, circa January 1952.
                                                          [*Aeroplane*

Although withdrawn from Bomber Command in 1945, the Lancaster's famous wartime partner, the Handley Page Halifax soldiered on with Coastal Command in the general reconnaissance role until March 1952, the last unit to use the type being No. 224 Squadron, one of whose GR.6s is seen here on a sortie from its base on Gibraltar.

Nocturnal Vampire. Crew of a de Havilland Vampire N.F.10 of No. 25 Squadron prepares to take off from West Malling, Kent, on a night exercise in 1952. A total of 95 Vampire N.F.10s were built and they were also used by several other squadrons pending the arrival of Meteor and Venom night fighters.

Avro Shackleton M.R.1 long-range maritime reconnaissance aircraft of the School of Anti-Submarine Warfare, R.A.F. Coastal Command, meets up with its quarry during a training exercise in 1952. The 'Shack' as it is known to the crews, first entered service in 1951 and as well as supplanting Coastal's veteran Lancasters it equipped new units with the expansion of the Command.

Supplementing the Shackleton in Coastal Command from 1952 to 1957 was the Lockheed Neptune, over 50 of which were obtained on loan under the American military aid programme for Europe. This one, photographed in May 1952, was from No. 217 Squadron, Kinloss, Morayshire.

Airspeed Oxford IIs of No. 9 Advanced Flying Training School, Welles-bourne Mountford, War-wickshire, in echelon formation in June 1952. The 'Ox-Box' was then standard equipment at the A.F.T.S.s of the R.A.F. where National Service officers completed their flying instruction to 'wings' standard, the last examples eventually being withdrawn in 1954.

R.A.F. aircraft have made many goodwill tours since the war, one of the most outstanding being the 24,000-mile tour of South America by Canberra B.2s of No. 12 Squadron in October 1952 — a trip which included the first jet crossing of the South Atlantic in both directions. Here one of No. 12's Canberras gives a flying demonstration over the famous beaches at Rio de Janeiro.

During the late 1940s and the 1950s aircraft of the R.A.F. Flying College at Manby, Lincs, made numerous navigational training flights over the North Pole—a featureless area where magnetic compasses are unreliable. The aircraft sometimes operated from bases within the Arctic Circle, and it was at one of these—R.C.A.F. base Resolute Bay—that this picture of a Hastings was taken early in 1953 at the end of an 11 hour flight.

Pending the arrival of British swept-wing jet fighters the R.A.F. acquired some 430 Canadair-built F-86E Sabres in 1952/53 and between then and mid-1966 these served in both the U.K. and Germany. Here Sabres are seen lined up at Bluie West One, Greenland, during the transatlantic ferry operation *Bechers Brook* performed by a unit of Transport Command.

Above: Most widely-used R.A.F. basic trainer between 1948 and 1953 was the Percival Prentice which succeeded the veteran Tiger Moth in Flying Training Command and remained standard equipment until the arrival of the Provost. This pair of Prentices sport the insignia of the Central Flying School and were photographed circa early 1953.

Right: Star performer at many air displays in the early 1950s was the Meteor T.7 aerobatic team of No. 203 Advanced Flying School, R.A.F. Driffied, Yorks—seen here climbing to start a formation loop. The Meteor T.7 first entered service in December 1948 and was the R.A.F.'s first jet trainer.

Below: Boulton Paul Balliol T.2 advanced trainers of No. 7 Flying Training School, Cottesmore— the only F.T.S. equipped with the type—practise formation flying in January 1953. The Balliol later served at the R.A.F. College, Cranwell, until superseded by the Vampire T.11 early in 1956.

W.R.A.F. at work: Since the war the Women's Royal Air Force (formerly the W.A.A.F.) has remained an important element of the Service. Scores of trades have been open to recruits, including surface worker (shown giving beauty treatment to a Meteor T.7) ...

... medical orderly (rescuing a 'victim' from the scene of a 'crash'—by the way, the Halifax nose no longer exists so it cannot be saved for the R.A.F. Museum!) ...

. . . operations clerk (signalling with an Aldis lamp to the pilot of a Meteor F.8) . . .

. . . and safety equipment worker
—typified by these W.A.A.F.'s
seen checking a dinghy and its
'K' rations at R.A.F. Feltwell.

Right: In July 1953 H.M. The Queen reviewed a vast gathering of men and machines from all Commands of the Service at R.A.F. Odiham, Hants. Here, Armstrong Whitworth Meteor N.F.11s of No. 29 Squadron bunch in interlocking V-formations over rows of parked Meteors, Shackletons, Valettas and Canberras during the climax of a full-scale rehearsal of the fly-past.

Armourers install a 20mm gun in the dorsal turret of a Shackleton M.R.2 at R.A.F. St. Eval, Cornwall, in June 1953.

Hucks starter is connected to a Bristol Fighter during rehearsals at Earls Court for the R.A.F. Pageant of Progress event at the 1953 Royal Tournament. The 'Brisfit' represented the inter-war years and included in the photo are servicing personnel in tropical uniform and a Trojan van.

Right: Part of the impressive scene at Odiham on the day of the Royal Review.

In May 1953 H.R.H. The Duke of Edinburgh gained his pilot's 'wings' after a course of instruction on R.A.F. Chipmunk and Harvard aircraft at White Waltham. Here he is seen about to take off from White Waltham on a solo flight in his five-starred Harvard, KF729.

In October 1953 this Canberra P.R.3—WE139—flown by Flt. Lt. R. L. Burton (*left*) and navigated by Flt. Lt. D. H. Gannon, won the speed section of the London-New Zealand Air Race by flying from London Airport (Heathrow) to Christchurch, a distance of 12,270 miles, in 23 hr. 51 min. The aircraft remained in service until 1969 when it was presented to the R.A.F. Museum.

An early postwar R.A.F. navigation trainer was the Handley Page Marathon T.11, adapted from passenger aircraft originally ordered by B.E.A. Twenty-eight Marathons were supplied to the R.A.F. in 1953/54 but by June 1958 they had all been retired from service.

Meteor F.8s of No. 500 (County of Kent) Squadron, R.Aux.A.F., over Valetta, Malta, during summer camp in 1953.

Engine fitters remove the Ghost engine from a Venom F.B.1 at the Central Fighter Establishment, West Raynham, Norfolk, in November 1953.

Firedog scenes, 1952. Preparing to take off on air strikes against the Malayan bandits, de Havilland Hornets of No. 33 Squadron and (*below*) a Bristol Brigand of No. 84 Squadron. Both types could carry mixed loads of rockets and bombs.

Above: R.A.F.'s 'Flying grocery boys' drop supplies by parachute to British security forces waiting near a jungle clearing (*ringed*) in Malaya during the Emergency.

Opposite, top. Airmen remove cameras from Spitfire P.R.19 PS890 of No. 81 Squadron, Malaya. To No. 81 fell the distinction of making the R.A.F.'s last operational sortie with a first-line Spitfire, the date of this memorable occasion being April 1, 1954, and the aircraft PS888.

Opposite, bottom: Sqn. Ldr. N. P. W. Hancock prepares to take off in his Hornet to make No. 33 Squadron's 5,000th strike against the terrorists, spring 1955.

From 1953 to 1955 the R.A.F. gave air support to the Kenya Government's ground forces in operations against the Kikuyu terrorist organisation known as the Mau Mau. The total R.A.F. force available was never anything but small and included Harvards, Lincolns, P.R. Meteors and a handful of transport and liaison aircraft. Two units involved during 1964 were No. 8 Squadron, detached from Aden, with Vampire F.B.9s (*right*) and No. 61 Squadron with Lincolns, detached from the U.K. (*below*).

Left: Busman's holiday. Slingsby Sky sailplane lands at R.A.F. Lyneham, Wilts, during a gathering there of clubs of the R.A.F. Gliding and Soaring Association circa 1954.

H

Above: Hunter fighters in production for the R.A.F. and other N.A.T.O. air forces at a Hawker Aircraft factory early in 1954. Rafts of wings fill up the foreground and lines of fuselage sections crowd the rear.

Opposite, top: Standard single-seat fighter of the R.A.F. from the mid 1950's until 1960 was the Hawker Hunter. First unit to be equipped—in 1954—was No. 43 Squadron which lost no time in producing the aerobatic team shown.

Opposite, bottom: Noteworthy in being the first jet aircraft on which R.A.F. pilots actually qualified for their 'wings' was the Vampire T.11 side-by-side two-seat advanced trainer which first entered service in 1952 with Advanced Flying Schools at Valley and Weston Zoyland. Seen here, in June 1954, are aircraft of No. 5 F.T.S. Oakington, first station to operate the second half of the Provost/Vampire sequence.

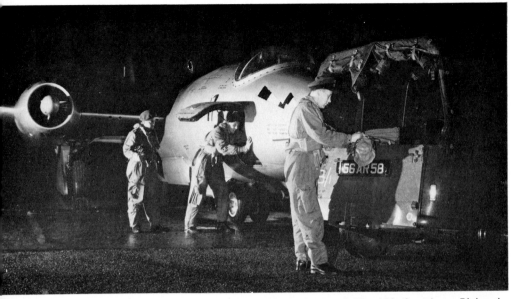

Crew of a Canberra of No. 101 Squadron, Binbrook, Lincs, prepare to board their aircraft for a night sortie in 1954. (*Below*) Pilot and observer in the cockpit of a Canberra. Third crew member, the navigator-plotter, was accommodated aft.

Hunting Percival Provost T.1s over the R.A.F. College, Cranwell, Lincs., in November 1954 shortly after having superseded the Chipmunk for basic training at the College. Elsewhere in Flying Training Command the Provost usually superseded the Prentice.

R.A.F.'s own Santa. And as might be expected he had a present for every guest when he appeared at this Christmas party at R.A.F. Ruislip, Middx, in December 1954.

Vampire Trainer fires a pair of 6-inch practice rockets at ground targets on a coastal range early in 1955.

First of Britain's four-jet V-bombers was the Vickers Valiant which entered squadron service early in 1955 when deliveries were made to No. 138 Squadron at Gaydon, Warwickshire. (*Right*) the twin Valiant production lines at Weybridge, Surrey. (*Below*) Valiant B.K.1 fitted with a nose probe for flight refuelling.

Youngsters inspect a Provost basic trainer at an R.A.F. station at a Battle of Britain Week 'at home' day.

Supermarine Swift F.1s and F.2s seen in 1955 wearing the red and white chequerboard markings of No. 56 Squadron, the only unit to fly the type as an interceptor fighter. Owing to serious technical difficulties the Swift had a very short stay in Fighter Command but subsequently, in its F.R.5 form, it proved more successful and equipped two fighter reconnaissance squadrons of the 2nd T.A.F. in Germany.

'Two silhouettes . . .' Artistic study of an R.A.F.
Whirlwind helicopter during a simulated air/sea
rescue mission.

Second T.A.F. Hunter aerobatic teams could compete with any of those in Fighter Command as this dramatic formation shot of Hunter F.4s from No. 93 Squadron at Jever in 1955 illustrates. Hunter 4s were employed on day fighter/ground attack duties in Germany and by 1956 equipped 13 squadrons there.

H.R.H. Princess Margaret meets Aircraft Apprentice 'Hamish McCrackers', the apprentices' pony mascot, at a passing out parade at No. 1 Radio School, Locking, Somerset, in July 1955.

Ground tradesman in the electrical and instrument engineering trade group learns primary servicing of Meteor instruments at R.A.F. Melksham, Wilts, in May 1955.

Canberra B.2s of No. 100 Squadron from Wittering, Northants, on a sortie over East Anglia in October 1955.   [*Flight International*

Two members of the Service enjoy a sightseeing tour in Aden's Arab quarter in November 1955. As events have since shown the natives did not continue to remain friendly !

In 1955 Auster A.O.P.9 two/three-seat air observation post or light liaison air-craft began operations against the Malayan terrorists with No. 656 Squadron, R.A.F. First sortie was flown by WZ670 seen here, on a leaflet-dropping mis-sion, and before handing over to the Army the squadron made over 143,000 *Firedog* operations.

December 15, 1955, saw the last operational sortie by a front-line Mosquito unit when Mosquito P.R.34 RG314 of No. 81 Squadron, Seletar, (illustrated) reconnoitred a terrorist hideout in the Malayan jungle.

The interceptor Hunter swoops to attack with its Aden
cannon a drogue sleeve target towed by a Meteor.

XB284

Largest aircraft to serve with the R.A.F. at the time of its introduction in March 1956, the Blackburn Beverley medium-range, high-capacity transport continued in service until the end of 1967 when it was supplanted by the Hercules. Beverleys were used both at home and overseas and the picture shows two aircraft of No. 47 Squadron—the original Beverley unit—at Abingdon, Oxon, in its early days. Unique features included a payload of nearly 22 tons, a freight hold of nearly 6,000 cu. ft., a passenger-carrying tail boom and remarkably short take-off and landing runs.

de Havilland Venom N.F.2 night fighters of 33 Squadron, Driffield, Yorkshire, early in 1956. The Venom N.F.2 entered service in 1953 and the N.F.3 which followed it was the last of the interim jet night-fighters (adapted from earlier day-fighter types) to enter R.A.F. service pending the introduction of the Gloster Javelin all-weather fighter.

Opposite, top: Meteor N.F.11 of No. 96 Squadron, 2nd Tactical Air Force, takes off from Ahlhorn, Germany, early in 1956. The N.F.11 was then the 2nd T.A.F.'s standard all-weather fighter, and 96 Squadron shared Ahlhorn with Nos. 213 and 256 Squadrons.

Above: Aircraft dispersal pens at R.A.F. Geilenkirchen, Germany, photographed in May 1956 when the airfield was the home of some Hunter, Sabre and Swift squadrons of 2nd T.A.F.

Opposite, bottom: Two members of No. 9 Squadron have a last snowball fight by the tails of their Canberra B.2s before leaving Binbrook, Lincs, in January 1956 for a tour of West Africa—where the natives called their aircraft 'steam chickens!'

Instructor at No. 3 Flying Training School, Feltwell, Norfolk, explains landing procedure to a student pilot prior to a flight in a Provost, March 1956.

Cranwell cadets training as navigators board a Vickers Valetta 'flying classroom' in 1956.

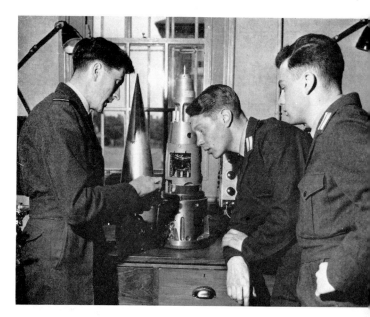

Intricate electronics system of a guided missile is explained to two R.A.F. technical cadets at Henlow . . .

. . . while another cadet studies airflow around a lifting surface in a wind tunnel.

Above: Technical cadets at Henlow are briefed before making training flights in Chipmunk aircraft, May 1956.

Opposite: Still an important source of recruits for the R.A.F. is the Air Training Corps whose training activities include flying experience both in powered gliders and aircraft. *Top:* A Cadet solos in a Slingsby Prefect. *Bottom:* An obviously satisfied customer pictured after a 'flip' in an R.A.F. Chipmunk elementary trainer.

Left: Unusual view of Buckingham Palace and The Mall seen from the last aircraft but one of a Shackleton formation (six aircraft from Nos. 42 and 206 Squadrons) during a special fly-past on June 21, 1956, to mark H.M. The Queen's birthday.

Vertical 'bomb burst' by Canberra T.4s of No. 231 Operational Conversion Unit, Bassingbourne, Cambs, during practice for the Coventry Air Pageant in July 1956.

Left: Navigator of the Comet 2 of No. 216 Squadron, Lyneham, Wilts, which took the Secretary of State for Air to Moscow for the Soviet Union's Air Display at Tushino in June 1956 checks route documents before take-off.

No. 49 Squadron Valiant which, on October 11, 1956, dropped Britain's first operational atomic bomb in trials over Maralinga, Southern Australia. On May 15, 1957, another of No. 49's Valiants test-dropped Britain's first operational H-bomb over Christmas Island.

Hunter F.4 of No. 130 Squadron, Bruggen, on show at Dreux airbase, in October 1956.

Goodbye to the Lanc. Last Lancaster in R.A.F. service—M.R.3 RF325—leaves the School of Maritime Reconnaissance, St. Mawgan, Cornwall, for the breaker's yard at Wroughton after a farewell ceremony on October 15, 1956. When reminded of such occasions one cannot help thinking how short-sighted the authorities were in allowing such wonderful relics to be destroyed.

Suez Crisis 1956. *Above:* Valiants and Canberras detached from their bases in Britain, parked on Luqa airfield, Malta, in November 1956. *Right:* Armourers prepare to load high-explosive bombs into a Canberra B.2 of No. 12 Squadron at Hal Far, Malta, prior to a raid on military installations in Egypt.

Two Hunter squadrons took part in the Suez campaign—Nos. 1 and 34 which operated their F.5s from Nicosia, Cyprus. The Hunter nearest the camera is from No. 34 Squadron and behind it is one of No. 1's machines.

Troops of the Gloucester Regiment practise rapid disembarkation from a hovering Bristol Sycamore helicopter during training in Cyprus for anti-terrorist operations, March 1957. The Sycamore was the first British-designed helicopter to enter R.A.F. service at home and overseas, initial deliveries being made in 1953—to St. Mawgan, Cornwall.

Another British designed and built helicopter which entered R.A.F. service in the 1950s, albeit in much smaller numbers than the Sycamore, was the Saro Skeeter. A two-seat light helicopter, it was used for training duties, initial deliveries being made circa 1957.

de Havilland Comet C.2s of No. 216 Squadron are serviced in a hangar at Lyneham circa early 1957. Ten Comet 2s (including two trainer aircraft) were supplied to 216 Squadron and they brought the most distant part of the Commonwealth within two days' travelling of the U.K. and the Far East within 24 hours.

V.I.P. de Havilland Devon of the Metropolitan Communications Squadron pictured on a north-westerly heading over the Thames, with Greenwich Power Station and the Royal Naval College below, in 1957. This unit, which was at Hendon until October 1957, flew a variety of aircraft including the Devon, Anson and Chipmunk.

Hunting Provost aerobatic team of the Central Flying School makes a snappy take-off from Little Rissington in July 1957 and (*below*) seconds later the pilot of the 'box' aircraft gets this view of the leader as he completes a loop. C.F.S. staff instructors are all pilots who have done a tour with operational squadrons and have served as instructors at one of the flying training schools. After the stiffest possible test, pupils graduate as C.F.S. qualified instructors— the highest piloting distinction in the world.

Gloster Javelin FAW.4s lined up on the runway at Tangmere, September 1957, ready to take part in a fly-past at the Farnborough Air Show. The Javelin was the first twin-jet delta-wing fighter in the world and entered R.A.F. squadron service in February 1956.

"... and pass the ammunition!" 30 mm ammunition for the Aden guns of a Javelin FAW.4 of No. 141 Squadron is checked over in the station armoury at Coltishall, Norfolk, in July 1957.

Javelin FAW.4 of No. 151 Squadron, Leuchars, formates with a Valetta of the Javelin Mobile Conversion Unit over the Firth of Forth in August 1957, when the J.M.C.U. was converting No. 151 from the Meteor night-fighter.

Spitfire 19 of the R.A.F.'s Battle of Britain Flight arrives at Biggin Hill from Duxford on July 11, 1957, to be made ready to take part in the annual fly-past over London in September.

Dedication of a font presented by the R.A.F. Association for the Battle of Britain commemorative chapel at Biggin Hill on Battle of Britain Sunday—September 15—1957. Seen in the picture are the Spitfire and Hurricane aircraft which are now permanently on view in front of the chapel right alongside the public highway.

Mechanics fit a 100-gallon plastic drop tank beneath the wing of a Hunter F.5 of No. 1 Squadron in 1957.

Vickers Valetta of the Air Supply Force, R.A.F. Far East, drops supplies to troops and police in the Malayan jungle circa early 1958. The Valettas were not often blessed with such an open dropping zone as this ; in many cases the clearings were almost inaccessible valleys. the mountains of which were often in cloud.   [Aeroplane

Plan view of a Hunter T.7 two-seat advanced trainer—a type which first entered R.A.F. service in 1958.

Venom F.B.4 of No. 8 Squadron, Khormaksar, Aden, with a special sun canopy over the pilot's cockpit early in 1958. Venoms took an important part in the R.A.F. operations in Oman in 1957.

The R.A.F.'s three types of V-bomber—the Valiant, the Vulcan and
the Victor—seen together early in 1958.

Mechanics at work on one of the main undercarriage units of a
Valiant.

Technician inspects the air-brakes of a Victor B.1 at the Aeroplane and Armament Experimental Establishment, Boscombe Down, Wilts. This particular aircraft was then on the strength of the Handling Squadron whose task it is to assess new Service types and compile the official Pilot's Notes and other instructional material.

Looking like the captain of a manned rocket—crew member in the bomb-aimer's position of a No. 232 Operational Conversion Unit Victor. The projecting tube is not a flight-refuelling probe, as some people might imagine, but the feed intake for the power controls.

At the R.A.F. College at Cranwell in Lincolnshire, cadets are trained for permanent commissions as officers. This view shows the 72nd entry of cadets marching past the reviewing officer at the passing-out parade on April 1, 1958.

Dining-in night at Cranwell. Cadets in the College dining hall.

The well-stocked library at the R.A.F. College, Cranwell. Note the portrait of Col. T. E. Lawrence—'Lawrence of Arabia'—who was himself once stationed at Cranwell, as readers of his autobiographical work 'The Mint' will know.

At the end of the current term at the R.A.F. College, the Air Council awards the Sword of Honour to the cadet who has shown the greatest merit in all categories of training. Here one proud winner of this coveted trophy poses for the camera beneath a painting of Lord Trenchard, 'Father of the R.A.F.'.

Up to the time of withdrawal in 1967 the R.A.F. played a key role in the policing of the hinterland of Aden, as part of the general pacification of the South Arabian and Persian Gulf areas. Here a Hunting Pembroke, used on casualty evacuation duties, stands at readiness on the 850 yards-long Dhala airstrip during operations near the Aden-Yemeni border in 1957.

Opposite: Brigand swan-song. Specially-equipped versions of the Bristol Brigand light bomber, designated T.4 and T.5, were employed by No. 238 Operational Conversion Unit on the initial training of radar navigators for night fighter duties from July 1951. These two pictures—both showing T 5s—were taken in March 1958 on the occasion of the farewell fly-past at North Luffenham, Rutland, where No. 238 O.C.U. disbanded.

[*lower photo Philip J. R. Moyes*

Opposite top: Important element of Britain's nuclear deterrent from 1958 until 1963 was the Douglas Thor intermediate-range ballistic missile force based in East Anglia and under the control of R.A.F. Bomber Command. The missiles were supplied to Britain by the United States and ferried across the Atlantic in U.S.A.F. transport aircraft.

From 1958 Bristol-Ferranti Bloodhound 1 radar-homing surface-to-air missiles were deployed in 16 Air Defence Missile Squadrons of Fighter Command in defence of V-bomber or Thor I.R.B.M. bases. Here a Valiant B.K.1 of No. 214 Squadron at Marham, Norfolk, is towed past some of the Bloodhound missiles protecting its base.

Opposite bottom: Thor I.R.B.M. is raised to the firing position on its launcher at R.A.F. Feltwell, Norfolk. The Thor force comprised 20 squadrons (each equipped with two missiles) and was maintained at constant readiness.

Canberra B.2 of No. 249 Squadron, from Akrotiri, Cyprus, pictured at El Adem, Libya, in September 1958. Some damage is noticeable at the rear end of the bomb doors; it was probably caused by stones while landing on the desert airfield.

Hunter F.6s of No. 208 Squadron and a Hastings of No. 70 Squadron on the airfield at Amman, Jordan, during the closing stages of the airlift, in October-November 1958, for British Forces being withdrawn from Jordan.

In December 1958 air reinforcements consisting of Whirlwind helicopters, Chipmunk and Pioneer aircraft were flown out to Cyprus to aid the British ground forces in their anti-EOKA terrorist operations. Here Chipmunks of No. 114 Squadron are seen on a reconnaissance sortie over the rough Cyprus countryside.

Scottish Aviation Pioneer of No. 209 Squadron is refuelled at Fort Sheen, Malaya, in March 1959. F.E.A.F. Pioneers, then operating as 267 Squadron, took part in the *Firedog* campaign against the Malayan terrorists, flying on internal security work and keeping the widely scattered jungle forts supplied. Later, as No. 267 Squadron, they saw action during the Brunei campaign. Pioneers also did much good work in Aden and Cyprus.

Responsible for much of the photographic reconnaissance in support of the *Firedog* campaign was No. 81 Squadron which between 1950 and 1959 flew more than 9,000 operational sorties—and many more were to follow. Here Sqn. Ldr. R. J. Linford, then the C.O., gets ready for a sortie over Malaya in his Meteor P.R.10 at Tengah, Singapore, in March 1959.

Victor scramble at Cottesmore, Rutland, June 1959. Aircraft is a B.Mk.1 of No. 15 Squadron.

Javelin FAW.7 of No. 64 Squadron and two Hunter F.6s of No. 65 Squadron fly over their base at Duxford, Cambs.—then Fighter Command's oldest operational station—in May 1959. The Spitfire parked alongside the control tower reminded visitors that Duxford was the first Spitfire station. [*Aeroplane*

Three thoroughbreds from the same stable. A Gloster Gladiator in echelon formation with a Gloster Meteor N.F.14 and a Gloster Javelin FAW4 in 1959. The Gladiator, then owned by the manufacturer, is now the property of the Shuttleworth Trust, while another, non-flying, example is preserved in the R.A.F. Museum.

Treble-One Squadron—then the R.A.F.'s premier aerobatic team—shows its prowess as it flies its black-painted Hunter F.6s over the V.I.P.s in the President's enclosure at the 1959 Farnborough Air Display.

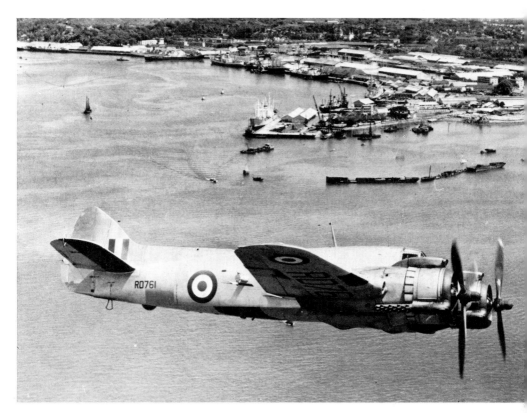

Beau's last bow. Beaufighter TT.10 RD761, from Seletar, Singapore, makes the R.A.F.'s final Beaufighter sortie on May 17, 1960

Retired just a year before the Beaufighter was the equally famous Sunderland. This event also took place at Seletar, the last aircraft to be withdrawn being Sunderland DP199 of No. 205 Squadron, and the date of the farewell flight May 15, 1959. During the *Firedog* campaign in Malaya, R.A.F. Sunderlands, each carrying 200 fragmentation bombs, took part in attacks on Communist terrorists.

Budding fliers arrive at the R.A.F. Aircrew Selection Centre at Hornchurch, Essex, in 1960.

French Air Force Dassault Super Mystère, temporarily based at R.A.F. Wattisham for the state visit of President de Gaulle in April 1960, flies in formation with a Javelin of No. 41 Squadron and a Hunter of No. 111 Squadron—then 'The Black Arrows' aerobatic team.

Guided missile fitters mount a Firestreak air-to-air guided missile on the wing pylon of a Javelin of No. 25 Squadron at Waterbeach, Cambs, in 1960.

Multi-purpose S.T.O.L. light transport which entered R.A.F. service in 1958—the Scottish Aviation Twin Pioneer. Eminently suitable for small airstrips (300 yards by 100 feet) in rough territory, it can carry 12 troops, or freight, or stretcher cases, and it is particularly noted for its work in Kenya (where this photo of a No. 21 Squadron machine was taken in 1960), Aden and the Far East.

Shackleton of No. 42 Squadron, Coastal Command, drops a canister of letters from home to the cruiser H.M.S. *Gambia* off the north-west coast of Spain, on her way home from the Far East in July 1960. The mail delivery was part of an air-sea exercise.

R.A.F.'s first true supersonic fighter was the English Electric (now B.A.C.) Lightning which replaced the Hawker Hunter in the squadrons of Fighter Command. First squadron was No. 74—'The Tigers'—two of whose F.1s are seen here soon after unit received the type in 1960.

Unique formation of R.A.F. aircraft brought together as a curtain-raiser for the 1960 Battle of Britain Week. From left to right they are :—Hurricane IIC, Spitfire P.R.19, Meteor F.8, Hunter F.6, Javelin FAW.9 and Lightning F.1.

Canberra B.(I)8 of No. 6 Squadron banks over the German countryside during a sortie from Laarbruch in the summer of 1960.

Opposite: F.E.A.F. visitor. Bomber Command Victor B.1 of No. 10 Squadron from Cottesmore, Rutland, flies low over the Malayan coast during a mobility exercise in the Far East in November 1960.

All in a day's work—1. An alsatian guard-dog gets a firm grip on his 'victim' during an exercise at an R.A.F. Police dog-handling school.

All in a day's work—2. Underwater ejection trials in progress at the Acceleration and Escape Section of the Institute of Aviation Medicine, Farnborough, in September 1960.

Opposite: Flying postman. Westland Whirlwind of No. 22 (Helicopter Search and Rescue) Squadron from R.A.F. Valley prepares to deliver Christmas mail to the keepers of Skerries Lighthouse off the Isle of Anglesey in December 1960.

In 1961, the year following that in which it re-equipped with Lightnings, No. 74 Squadron performed wing-overs and rolls with nine aircraft in tight formation. It was the first aerobatic team
to fly Mach 2 aircraft and in 1962 it had the leading role as 'The Tigers'.

Opposite: 'Treble One' Squadron's Lightning F.1As demonstrate their remarkable climb performance as they scorch their way skywards over Laffans Plain during the 1961 Farnborough Air Show.

[*Aeroplane*

Opposite, top: Valiant B.(K.)1 tanker of No. 214 Squadron refuels a Vulcan B.2. Flight re-fuelling plays an important part in giving the V-force extended range for operations and overseas deployment and the premature retirement of the Valiant in 1964, following the discovery of dangerous metal fatigue in the airframe, was a serious handicap, until Victor tankers became available in quantity.

Salute to a veteran. A Vulcan B.2 of No. 617 Squadron, roars up from the runway over its famous forebear, the Avro Lancaster permanently displayed alongside the main gate at R.A.F. Scampton, Lincs.

Opposite, bottom: Missile the R.A.F. never got. Full-scale dummy round of the Douglas Sky-bolt air-launched nuclear missile fitted beneath the wing of a Vulcan B.2. Originally nominated as the replacement for the cancelled Blue Streak L.R.B.M., Skybolt was in turn abandoned by the British Government in favour of the Polaris submarine-launched I.R.B.M.

The C.O. and two fellow pilots of the famous No. 56 Squadron get to work on plastic model aircraft for the unit's museum.

Officers and N.C.O.'s get the latest 'gen' in the aircraft recognition room at an R.A.F. station.

Apprentices winch the gun pack into the belly of an old, ex-74 Squadron, Hawker Hunter at R.A.F. Halton, Bucks, under the watchful eye of an instructor.

Traditional scene at Halton as aircraft apprentices celebrate following passing-out parade on completion of their training.

Opposite, top: On completion of 25 years' continuous service, or sometimes on special Royal recommendation, op - erational R.A.F. squadrons become eligible for the award of a silk standard on which is embroidered their official badge and some of their battle honours. Shown is the standard awarded to No. 205 Squadron.

Opposite, bottom: When R.A.F. squadrons are disbanded it is not unusual for their standards to be laid-up in local churches until such time as they might be re-formed. Such was the case when No. 100 Squadron disbanded at Wittering, Northants, in 1959. Following its re-formation there in 1962 it reclaimed its standard from the church at nearby Stamford, Lincs, and the occasion was marked by a special ceremony including a parade watched by the Mayor of Stamford and other civil dignitaries.

Men of an R.A.F. mountain rescue team lower a 'casualty' down a snow-covered mountainside in the Ben Nevis area during a training exercise in February 1963. These teams have been responsible for saving many lives, of both Servicemen and civilians.

Close-up of the B.A.C. Bloodhound 2 surface-to-air missile which succeeded the Bloodhound 1 in the R.A.F. and was deployed in Malaysia from 1964. It has a higher performance, is more immune to counter-measures and is air-transportable.

Ballistic Missile Early Warning System. The B.M.E.W.S. station at Fylingdales, on the Yorkshire Moors. Opened in 1963, this station can give early warning to the V-force so that it could scramble and escape destruction on the ground and make an immediate retaliatory strike against enemy targets.

Vulcan B.2s on their O.R.P.s (Operational Readiness Platforms) angled into the side of the runway at their base in Lincolnshire to speed 'scrambling'.

On the Rock. Armourers load depth charges into a Shackleton M.R.3 of No. 224 Squadron on North Front Airfield, Gibraltar, during N.A.T.O. exercise *Dawn Breeze* in March 1962.

Down memory lane. Typical of many abandoned R.A.F. airfields dotted up and down Britain is Full Sutton, Yorks, once a wartime bomber station and, in more recent times, a Thor I.R.B.M. base. When this picture was taken, in July 1963, sheep strayed in and out of this old Nissen hut and grass and weeds flourished all around.

[*Yorkshire Evening Press*

Much in evidence in and around Aden were the Westland Belvederes of No. 26 Squadron, which also had its headquarters there. The Belvederes operated from the Royal Navy carrier *Centaur* to lift commandos into Tanganyika (now Tanzania) during the rebellion in 1963 and subsequently helped support the Army in the Radfan operations in South Arabia.

Airman marshalls a Lightning F.2 of No. 19 Squadron during night flying at R.A.F. Leconfield, Yorks, in July 1963. Only one other squadron received Lightning 2s—No. 92, which was No. 19's sister squadron at Leconfield. Later both squadrons were assigned to 2nd T.A.F., in Germany, and became the first Lightning units to be permanently stationed overseas.

H.M. The Queen visits R.A.F. Thorney Island on July 27, 1964, in a Hawker Siddeley Andover C.C.2 of The Queen's Flight.

Some of the worst flying conditions in the world are to be found in Aden, but these did not deter the Beverleys of No. 84 Squadron which were based for several years at R.A.F. Khormaksar. Much of their flying was to up-country airstrips of the Federal Regular Army, at many of which there was only a short rolled-sand runway. Here a ghost-like Beverley of No. 84 Squadron disappears in a swirling cloud of dust during its landing run at one of the up-country airstrips in Aden in 1963.

Vulcan B.2 of No. 617 Squadron—the 'Dambusters'—armed with a Blue Steel stand-off bomb.

No, not spacemen but groundcrew wearing special clothing necessary for protection against the dangerous fuel which powers Blue Steel.

Hunter F.G.A.9 of No. 8 Squadron from Khormaksar, Aden, over the Radfan, the mountainous area west of Aden bordering on the Yemen, in November 1964. Earlier in the year the ground-attack Hunters were continuously in action in the Radfan against local tribesmen who staged an armed revolt. Co-operation between the Hunters and the forward troops, for whom they provided close-support, reached such a pitch of efficiency that troops in the forward areas were calling down the Hunters to strike the tribesmen's mountain strongholds only 25 yards from their own positions.

Hastings Met.1 of No. 202 Squadron from Aldergrove makes the R.A.F.'s final long-range weather reconnaissance sortie over the Atlantic in August 1964. Since then this weather service, which benefits many other countries besides Britain, has been provided by space satellites and the many airliners crossing the Atlantic daily.

Men of No. 33 (Field) Squadron, R.A.F. Regiment, defend Thumier airstrip, Aden, in 1964.

Russian Mya-4 (N.A.T.O. code-name 'Bison') bombers often visit the coastal regions of Britain and when they do they are intercepted by R.A.F. Lightnings. *Below*, Firestreak-armed Lightnings of No. 74 Squadron escort from British airspace a Bison intercepted at 37,000 ft., 100 miles beyond the coast.

To prove the validity of the V.T.O.L. strike and reconnaissance concept for military use, a tripartite trials squadron, equipped with Hawker Siddeley Kestrels and comprising British, German and American pilots, operated at R.A.F. West Raynham, Norfolk, in 1964/65. As a result of these trials the Harrier, the operational derivative of the Kestrel, was ordered for the R.A.F. *Right,* some of the Kestrels at West Raynham, sporting their special tripartite markings. *Below,* an R.A.F. pilot and other members of the squadron admire their feathered mascot.

Ghost riders in the sky. Strange patterns caused by gases from the twin 30-mm Aden cannon of a 'Treble One' Squadron Lightning 1A during an armament practice sortie from Wattisham, Suffolk, in 1965.

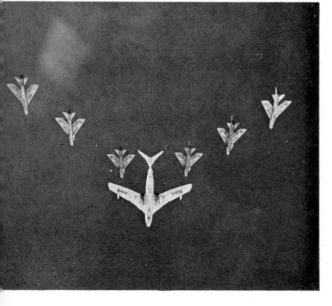

'Hurry up, chaps—we've got a new barman!' Early Victor K.1A tanker flies over the North Sea on flight refuelling trials with Lightning F.2s of No. 19 Squadron from Lecon-field, Yorks, in 1965. Six of these tankers using a '2-point' system, as seen, were delivered to the R.A.F. and they provided interim flight re-fuelling capability pending the build up of the '3-point' Victor tanker force.

H.R.H. The Duke of Edinburgh, accompanied by the station commander, makes a tour of inspection at R.A.F. Labuan in March 1965 during the confrontation in Borneo.

French paratroopers and Sandhurst officer cadets embark on a Wessex H.C.2 of No. 72 Squadron, Transport Command, during an exercise at Thetford, Norfolk, in May 1965.

First jet-powered navigation trainer designed specifically for such a purpose to enter R.A.F. service was the Hawker Siddeley Dominie T.1 which became operational in October 1965 at No. 1 Air Navigation School, Stradishall, Suffolk. *Left:* interior of a Dominie showing a trainee navigator receiving instruction (compare this photo with that on page 132 of Volume 2 of this work) and, *below,* a Dominie at Stradishall.

View from a Gnat Trainer of 'The Red Arrows' during a rehearsal in September 1965—their first season. Flown by instructors of the C.F.S., the red-painted Gnats have earned acclaim both in Britain and in many other countries in Europe, and at the time of writing they remain the R.A.F.'s premier aerobatic team.

Thermometer registers 30° below zero at Andya air base on the edge of the Arctic in Norway as a Hunter of No. 54 Squadron, normally based at West Raynham, is marshalled on to the runway during N.A.T.O. exercise *Winter Express* early in 1966.

Two Beagle Basset C.C.1 light communications aircraft of the Northern Communications Squadron, based at Topcliffe, formate over the Yorkshire countryside. Twenty Bassets have been supplied to the R.A.F., the first examples going to the above-mentioned unit at Topcliffe in 1965.

Whirlwind H.A.R.10's of the Central Flying School pictured during an exercise in February 1966.

Canberra T.11—conversion of the B.2 for the training of A.I radar operators—of No. 85 Squadron, Binbrook, Lincs, formates with a Lightning F.6 of No. 5 Squadron also from Binbrook, in 1966.

Troops embark in a VC10 of Transport Command at Akrotiri, Cyprus, during a mobility exercise.

Whirlwind helicopter is loaded into a Belfast at R.A.F. [Odiham, Hants, in late 1966. The Belfast can carry four partially dismantled Whirlwinds, alternative loads including three partially-dismantled Wessex helicopters, or two Polaris-type missiles.

Lightning F.2 of No. 19 Squadron, Gutersilöh, Germany, armed with Firestreak air-to-air missiles. As mentioned earlier, Nos. 19 and 92 Squadrons, were the first Lightning units to be permanently based overseas.

Canberra B.(I.)8 night intruder of No. 14 Squadron, Wildenrath, R.A.F. Germany, stands ready for instant action in 1967.

Men of the R.A.F. Regiment drive their vehicle out of the freight hold of a Hawker Siddeley Andover C.1 of No. 52 Squadron, Far East Air Force, at Seletar, Singapore, in March 1967.

In June 1967 Lightnings were based in the Far East for the first time when No. 74 Squadron flew to Tengah, Singapore, from Scotland to replace the Javelins of No. 64 Squadron. A Lightning F.6 of 'The Tigers' over the Singapore river.

Whirlwind 10 of No. 110 Squadron, F.E.A.F., escorts troops on the move on a road through the Malaysian jungle during exercise *Leary* in July 1968. No. 110 Squadron's Whirlwinds were the last aircraft to operate in Borneo in support of the Malaysian forces; they were finally withdrawn in November 1967, by which time they had flown nearly 25,000 sorties since 1962.

Opposite, top: Tiger man. No. 74 Squadron pilot gets a helping hand with his kit from his wife as he prepares to go off duty at Tengah.

Opposite, bottom: Dawn take-off for a Scottish Aviation Pioneer of No. 209 Squadron during Exercise *Gedgeley*, Malacca, June 1967. Pioneers of No. 209 were active during the Brunei campaign of 1962 to 1966, while those of another F.E.A.F. unit—No. 267 Squadron—played an important part in the *Firedog* operations against the Malayan terrorists.

Belvedere, of No. 66 Squadron, F.E.A.F., puts a cross on a church in Singapore in December 1966. This unit's Belvederes were active throughout the Brunei campaign of 1962-66, operating from Labuan in Borneo.

Whirlwind 10 of No. 103 Squadron from R.A.F. Seletar, winches down a sick berth attendant to H.M. Submarine *Andrew* in the China Sea after a 20-mile flight from Singapore.

Shackleton M.R.3 of No. 205 Squadron, F.E.A.F., makes a low pass over the Singapore waterfront during a patrol from its base at nearby Changi. It was a Shackleton crew of No. 205 which, during a daylight patrol in September 1964, spotted parachutes in the treetops around Labis, giving security forces their first proof that Indonesian regular troops had made an airborne landing on the Malaysian peninsular.

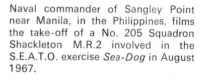

Naval commander of Sangley Point near Manila, in the Philippines, films the take-off of a No. 205 Squadron Shackleton M.R.2 involved in the S.E.A.T.O. exercise *Sea-Dog* in August 1967.

Salvo. Vulcan B.2 releases its full complement of 21 1,000-lb. medium-capacity bombs. Its contemporary, the Victor, could carry no fewer than 35 of these 'conventional' bombs.

Canberra B.15s of No. 45 Squadron, F.E.A.F., from Tengah, Singapore, on a sortie over the jungle. In 1962-66 this unit's B.6s took part in the Brunei campaign.

Vulcan B.2s of R.A.F. Strike Command fly in line astern after take off following a practice 'scramble' order. The V-Force was held at round-the-clock readiness and its quick re-action alert (Q.R.A.) and scramble time, along with its in-flight refuelling capability, ensured great mobility.

Hawker Hart Trainer K4972, whose remains were discovered in a barn in Cumberland in 1962, pictured in January 1968 during restoration at No. 4 School of Technical Training, St. Athan, Glam. The aircraft has since been almost fully restored to its original condition and is owned by the R.A.F. Museum which is to become permanently established at Hendon.

Nord A.S.30 air-to-ground guided missile is hoisted on to the wing pylon of a No. 45 Squadron Canberra B.15 at Labuan, Borneo, during Exercise *Hot Shot* in April 1968.

Warts an' all. Canberra T.17 electronic countermeasures (E.C.M.) trainer used for training air electronics officers (A.E.O.'s) for the V-force.

All together now. Four members of the R.A.F.'s famous 'Falcons' free-fall parachute team caught by the camera as they link hands for a stylish delayed drop. Formed in 1961—although it did not acquire its name until 1965—the team is drawn from R.A.F. instructors at No. 1 Parachute Training School, Abingdon, Berks.

Lightning T.5 two-seat supersonic trainer of No. 226 Operational Conversion Unit, Coltishall, Norfolk, inches from the runway at 150 m.p.h. plus.   [Peter R. March

Flying control room at No. 226 O.C.U.

April 1, 1968 marked the R.A.F.'s 50th anniversary. Climax of the Jubilee Year celebrations was the Royal Review at Abingdon, Oxon, on June 14—a display repeated the next day for the public—when many types of R.A.F. aircraft, past and present, were on view, and some 160 machines took part in the flying display. Here are two views of the static aircraft park taken during the rehearsals.

Opposite, top: Bristol Britannia C.2 from R.A.F. Lyneham, Wilts, formates with a Hercules C.1. The Britannia entered R.A.F. service in 1959 and since then has performed long-range strategic missions in many parts of the world, forming the basis for the rapid deployment of the Army's U.K. Strategic Reserve.

Westland Sioux of the Central Flying School, Ternhill—only R.A.F. unit to operate this light helicopter.

[*Peter R. March*

Whirlwind H.A.R.10 of Near East Air Force rescues an exhausted swimmer from the sea off the coast of Cyprus in 1968. R.A.F. search and rescue helicopters, operating both at home and abroad, save scores of lives each year and not infrequently their work is extremely hazardous.

Opposite, bottom: R.A.F. version of the Lockheed C-130E medium range transport is the Hercules C.1, 66 examples of which have been acquired to supplement the Argosy and replace the Hastings and Beverley. First squadron to receive the Hercules was No. 36 in August 1967.

'Faithful Annie'. One of the R.A.F.'s few surviving Avro Ansons photographed in 1968 in service as a communications hack with Air Support Command.

Opposite: Two more long-range strategic transports which originally served with Transport Command before it became Air Support Command are the B.A.C. VC10 C.1 (*above*) and the Short Belfast (*below*). The Belfast is notable in being the first British aircraft ever designed from the start for the long-range military transport role, while the VC10. C.1 has the distinction of being the heaviest aircraft ever to enter R.A.F. service. The VC10 in the picture is seen leaving Changi, Singapore, en route for the U.K. Five VC10 flights, each carrying up to 125 passengers, are operated to and from the Far East every week.

McDonnell Phantom FGR.2, one of 150 F-4M Phantoms ordered for the R.A.F. This particular example, XT891, was reportedly the first machine to be delivered to the Service (in August 1968) and began its career with No. 228 Operational Conversion Unit at Coningsby, Lincs, in September 1968. First operational Phantom squadron was No. 43—'The Fighting Cocks'—which began to receive FG.1 aircraft, originally ordered for the Royal Navy, in August 1969.

Being supplied to the R.A.F. as an interim Canberra replacement is the Hawker Siddeley Buccaneer S.20—first R.A.F. example delivered is shown. Retro-fitted ex-Fleet Air Arm aircraft are to be supplemented in R.A.F. service by 26 new aircraft and the first squadron, No. 12, re-formed at Honington in October 1969.

Scheduled to replace the piston-engined Shackleton M.R.2 for long-range shore-based maritime patrol duties is the Hawker Siddeley Nimrod, first examples of which entered service in 1969. Crew of the Nimrod numbers 11 men—two pilots, an engineer, two beam look-outs, two navigators, a radio operator, two sonar operators and a radar operator.

Jet Provost T.4 of the Central Flying School sporting R.A.F. Training Command's new red and white colour scheme in April 1969.
[Peter R. March]

Old stager still going strong is the Vickers Varsity which was the postwar replacement for the Wellington T.10 crew trainer. First deliveries were made to the R.A.F. in 1951 and several examples, such as this one from No. 5 F.T.S., Oakington, continue to give excellent service.   [Peter R. March]

Opposite, top: Sqn. Ldr. Tom Lecky-Thompson makes a vertical take-off in a Hawker Siddeley Harrier from a disused coal yard at St. Pancras Station, London, on May 5, 1969, during the Daily Mail Transatlantic Air Race. In the race Lecky-Thompson took the prize for the fastest overall time in the East-West direction. Another Harrier, flown by Sqn. Ldr. Graham Williams and entered for the West-East leg put up an even faster overall time between the Empire State Building and the G.P.O. Tower—5 hr. 49 min. 52 sec. The Harriers were refuelled by Victor tankers over the Atlantic.

Below: Drink, Sir? Harrier G.R.1 of No. 1
Squadron is refuelled in flight by a Victor
K.1A of No. 57 Squadron in 1969.

Harrier cockpit.

Two-seat operational training version of the Harrier G.R.1 is the T.2, which is some ten feet longer, with a second cockpit in tandem in an extended forward fuselage, a lengthened tail boom, and increased fin area. Thirteen are being supplied to the R.A.F. and they retain the full combat capability of the single-seater.